The Brown Girl's Guide To College

This Book Belongs To:

____

This book is dedicated:

to the Family that raised us,

the Educators that pushed us,

the Adversity that made us resilient,

to all the Brown Girls around the world who dream, and

to the Dream Giver.

Table of Contents

Greetings!

When we first began to write, we wanted to write to girls like us. Young, brown, full of dreams but with little guidance. We all grew up differently. We had people in our lives that loved us. People in our lives that wanted the best for us. But we had this vision. Something we saw when we closed our eyes.

The funny thing about writing a book is that you never really know who will pick your book up. So, whether you are young, old, brown, or white, dream or no dream, we hope this guide makes you see something when you close your eyes, or helps you be closer to what you see when you close your eyes.

The time is now for women of color around the world to go after what they want. The time is now for easy access to resources that help women of color. Grab your pen, highlighter, planner, and let's get to work.

Love always,

Taylor, Amber, Paige and Asia

Foreword

Hey, girl, hey! I hope you feel as good as you look today and in the case that you aren't feeling the best, don't fret. The assurance reading the *Browns Girl's Guide to College (The BGGC or The Guide)* will give you about your ability to do what many women of color have paved the way for you to do: secure that degree, will intensify your Brown Girl Magic glow from the inside out. And *that* my friend, should make you feel great, *really* great.

I met one of *The BGGC* authors, Taylor Flake, in 2016, when she was appointed to serve on a committee I chaired, Alpha Kappa Alpha Sorority, Inc.'s International Undergraduate Activities Committee (UAC). Taylor significantly contributed to committee efforts to galvanize nearly 8,000 undergraduate sorority members to "be of service to all mankind" around the world and graduate from college. All the while, she was simultaneously completing her senior year in college and preparing for law school. While working together on sub-committees tasked to develop a sophisticated, paid summer internship program for undergraduate students and raise scholarship funds, it became evident to me that Taylor understood the importance of pursuing career development opportunities, creating opportunities for others and associating herself with determined, conscious women ready to stand on the shoulders of those that came before them and help those following in their footsteps.

I met Amber, Paige, and Asia through Taylor. While being acquainted with these exemplary women, it became evident that they all have a genuine desire to provide a real, one-on-one, intimate discussion about what it takes for brown girls to make it through college. This desire jumps through the text as you make your way through the guide's lessons, questionnaires, and other activities feeling as if this guide was written specially for you. That's because it was.

In the words of one of the *The BGGC* writers, while you are working through *The Guide*, "you'll feel like you are talking to a big sister, a close friend, or your cool aunt." Inspired by their parents, Mae Jemison, and many other trailblazing people of color, Taylor, Amber, Paige, and Asia have left a seat at the table of brown girl graduates just for you.

When the ladies presented me with the opportunity to write the foreword for the first edition of *The Brown Girl's Guide to College*, I responded with great excitement and interest. Like all of *The BGCC's* authors, I am extremely passionate about making sure brown girls know they can succeed at college if that is what fulfilling their purpose in life entails.

As a woman of color, I know that women of color are worthy of being college-educated and that we are capable of being executive leaders, empowering people around the world despite what statistics and stereotypes suggest. In spite of common adversities faced by minorities, by age 22, I studied in China, served on the Board of Directors of a 50-million-dollar corporation (Alpha Kappa Alpha Sorority, Inc.),[1] traveled around the world empowering young girls and women, and was the only African-American to graduate from my Master of Accountancy class. I interned seven times throughout my college career. I have worked in Corporate America, the non-profit arena, and the public sector. At 23, I became a home and business owner. I plan to go to law school and eventually become a Supreme Court Justice and a CEO teaching other women how to advance their careers and find their passions. Having a college degree opened the door for every single one of these things to be possible and strengthened my ability to defy statistics and stereotypes.

If you're one of those people who have a burning desire to know the value of something before you even consider participating in the activity or in this case, reading through this amazing piece of work, I get you. I understand that your time is precious, girl, and that's exactly why you should read *The Brown Girls Guide to College.*

As you read *The Guide*, you'll not only learn strategies to make the most of your time throughout the *entire* college process (that means before you submit your application, during your time in school, and even after you graduate), you'll also complete a series of questionnaires and activities that will make this guide personal to you.

The BGGC is a gem. Here are just five of many things you will be prepared to do after reading *The Brown Girl's Guide to College:*

Find comfort in knowing that no matter how unfamiliar the college journey

1 http://aka1908.com/

ahead may seem to you, you are not alone on your journey – even in the times where you may be the only minority in the room. There is a bountiful community of women of color rooting for you around the world.

Understand the ins and outs of navigating the college process. From submitting your application to ordering your cap and gown, securing financial aid to balling on a college budget, choosing your major to pursuing career opportunities, managing your time to managing your sanity, transitioning from a teenager to a full blown adult, this Guide will supply the information you need to make wise decisions when it comes to all this and more.

Become knowledgeable about resources available to you and how to find those "not so easy to find" resources on campus.

Identify factors that will affect your ability to excel as a scholar and develop techniques to address those factors.

Approach your time in college with the confidence that you are capable of totally crushing the game and graduating on time if you are willing to put in the work and commit to the process.

I guarantee you this Guide will be the reads of reads, hunty!

Before going any further, I want to commend you for exploring the option to pursue post-secondary education through college and ask that you encourage your peers to do the same. As recently as five years ago, 31 million girls of primary age were out of school and 17 million were expected to never enter school.[2] Still in 2019, many girls around the world are stripped of the privilege to learn and here you are with the opportunity to go to college. The opportunity is yours to seize and *The Brown Girls Guide to* College is going to help you seize it.

Due to a number of factors that are usually beyond our control, minorities, especially women of color often times feel so intimidated by the college process that we choose not to apply out of fear or ignorance of the process. The 1992 New York Times Article "Minority Students Cite Bias in Higher-Education Quest," quotes Black, Hispanic, and American Indian students expressing feelings of discouragement from believing they can succeed in intellectually demanding professions. The article provides an account of Guy Bluford, the first black astronaut, being told by his high school adviser that he was "only smart enough for trade school."[3] Unfortunately, in 2019, majority of minorities have had similar

2 UNESCO, Educational For All Global Monitoring Report, October 2013, https://en.unesco.org/gem-report/sites/gem-report/files/girls-factsheet-en.pdf
3 Susan Chira, "Minority Students Cite Bias In Higher-Education Quest," New York Times, August

encounters with micro and macro aggressions. So, I applaud you for investing the time to learn more about the college process and planning to excel. If that part does not apply to you yet, let's change that right now.

Because women of color do not always get the recognition or, better yet, the mere acknowledgment we deserve on mainstream platforms, it is easy to feel like there are glass ceilings we have yet to shatter. When in all actuality, they have already been shattered for us and replaced with ladders to get to the next level. For many women of color, this myopia is what holds us back from moving forward when it comes to taking advantage of opportunities to pursue education and our further our careers. Fear not. As I said before, this opportunity is yours to seize.

If you are still on the fence about going to college or getting a professional degree, I need you to understand the value of a having a degree in the world we live in today. It is my hope that knowing the information being shared with you in this foreword will help you make informed decisions about your pursuit of higher education and encourage you to read *The Brown Girls Guide to College* even more.

While having a college degree is not the end all be all to determine whether you have a life of opportunity, unlike not having a college degree, it generally opens up more doors to opportunity than it closes. Whether you have a college degree can influence many aspects of life from home ownership to marriage and retirement. The primary benefit of a college degree is access to higher income and access to greater professional opportunities.

Simply put, there is a greater demand for educated workers in the global marketplace. Whether we like it or not, employers generally assess degree attainment as the most significant indicator of an applicant's level education and ability to learn. The higher level of education you obtain, the greater your economic advancement in America over those with lower levels of institutionalized education.

1992, https://www.nytimes.com/1992/08/04/us/minority-students-cite-bias-in-higher-education-quest.html

2017 Average Annual Salary Level By Education Level	
Less Than High School Diploma	$27,040
High School Diploma	$37,024
Some College, No Degree	$40,248
Associate's Degree	$43,472
Bachelor's Degree	$60,996
Master's Degree	$72,852
Professional Degree	$95,472
Doctorate	$90,636
Weekly Salary Obtained from U.S. Bureau of Labor Statistic][4] and multiplied by 52 weeks/year	

While your salary will depend on a number of factors like where you live, your work experience and so forth, under ideal, non-subjective circumstances, the primary attribute for your salary consideration will be your education level. As illustrated in the chart above, on average, there is nearly a $25,000 difference in annual income between that of a high school a college graduate with a bachelor's degree, a projected requirement for nearly 40% of employment opportunities by 2020.[5]

4 Elka Torpey, "Measuring the value of education," *Career Outlook,* U.S. Bureau of Labor Statistics, April 2018, https://www.bls.gov/careeroutlook/2018/data-on-display/education-pays.htm
5 Carnevale, Smith, and Strohl, "Recovery: Job Growth and Education Requirements Through 2020," Georgetown Public Policy Institute Center on Education and Workforce

If you think that difference in income isn't grave, just think about what you could do with an extra $25,000 in your bank account right now. Now imagine having a slew of responsibilities, presumably reasonably more than you have now, like a mortgage, children, tuition. Go ahead, add items as you see fit. Still think earning $25,000 more doesn't make a difference? Over time, this difference can equate to a salary gap of hundreds of thousands of dollars and significantly different lifestyles.

While education is considered to be the great equalizer by those who have not experienced marginalization, it is not some impenetrable shield women of color can depend on to avoid the grips of the gender pay gap. When it comes to salary offers and promotions, your gender (and color) comes into play. The gender pay gap starts early, so you need to know about it early in your career. Most employers have written policies asserting non-discriminatory methods when it comes to determining salary but as you probably know, when it comes to the treatment of minorities, the unwritten rules can trump what's in black and white creating areas of grey we have to learn to navigate. Fortunately, for you, the authors of *BGGC* touch on navigating grey areas as a minority in *The Guide.*

The gender pay gap also known as the wage gap has plagued almost every industry and field for centuries. Without getting too into specifics, the gender pay gap is the average difference between the remuneration for working men and women. In 2017, there was a 20% gender wage gap between female full-time, year-round workers and that of men with women making only 80.5 cents for every dollar earned by men.[6] In order to achieve gender parity, a woman would need to work an average of four extra months to catch up with her white male counterparts.

Let's bring this closer to home. According to a plethora of reputable sources like the Institute on Women's Policy Research and the Economic Policy Institute, women of color experience greater wage gaps than that of white women. According to CNBC, "Black women earn $0.63 for every dollar earned by their white male counterparts. Native American women earn $0.57 to every dollar, and Latina women earn $.054. Meanwhile, white and Asian women earn $0.79 and $0.87, respectively."[7] The fact of the matter is that women of color are evidently considered less valuable in the workforce than just about everyone else.

---

6 Institute for Women's Policy Research, "Pay Equity & Discrimination," https://iwpr.org/issue/employment-education-economic-change/pay-equity-discrimination/

7 Courtney Connley, "Reminder: Today Isn't Equal Pay Day for black, Latina, or Native American women" CNBC, April 2018. https://www.cnbc.com/2018/04/10/today-isnt-equal-pay-day-for-black-latina-or-native-american-women.html

Women of color face an even wider employment gap in corporate leadership roles. Per the Center for American Progress, as of 2015, we made up 35 percent of the female labor force and 16 percent of the total labor force, yet we accounted for less than four percent of executive or senior-level officials and managers and 0.4 percent of CEOs in S&P 500 companies. As recently as 2013, more than two –thirds of Fortune 500 companies had no women of color as board of directors at all.[8]

In the United States, women represent nearly half of the labor force, yet we are disproportionately underrepresented at managerial and executive levels in every sector, industry, and field. Earlier last year, I read a New York Times article stating that in 2018, there are fewer women in leadership positions than there are men named John.[9] The Center for American Progress reports that in the legal field, women are 45 percent of associates but only 22 percent of partners; in medicine, women comprise 37 percent of all physicians and surgeons but only 16 percent of permanent medical school deans; in academia, women are only 31 percent of full professors and 27 percent of college presidents.[10]

When it comes to U.S. politics, there is much progress to be made at every level. 2016 marked a year of many firsts for women of color including election of the first Latina member of the U.S. Senate and the first female senator of Nevada, Sen. Catherine Cortez Masto. Senator Kamala Harris became the first Indian American U.S. Senator and the second ever African-American Senator and Representative. Stephanie Murphy became the first Vietnamese American women elected to congress. Great strides indeed, but even with this progress, women of color represent only 38 of 535, just seven percent, of U.S. Congressional seats.[11]

While this may be your first time learning about the gender wage gap or gaps in senior level leadership, effects of both gaps have plagued pockets of minorities for centuries. Advances are certainly being made, but we are still so far behind where we need to be which is why you, yes *YOU,* should aim to be a part of the change.

Many women of color who have blazed trails in each of their respective fields

8 Judith Warner, "The Women's Leadership Gap," Center for American Progress, May 2017. https://www.americanprogress.org/issues/women/reports/2017/05/21/432758/womens-leadership-gap/
9 Miller, Quealy, Sanger-Katz, "The Top Jobs Where Women Are Outnumbered by Men Named John," New York Times, April 2018. https://www.nytimes.com/interactive/2018/04/24/upshot/women-and-men-named-john.html?mtrref=undefined&gwh=F019A621405B929440F47E4FCCD300DD&gwt=pay
10Judith Warner, "The Women's Leadership Gap," Center for American Progress, May 2017. https://www.americanprogress.org/issues/women/reports/2017/05/21/432758/womens-leadership-gap/
11 Rutgers Eagleton Institute of Politics, "Facts on Women of Color in Office," Center for American Women And Politics, 2018. http://www.cawp.rutgers.edu/fact-sheets-women-color

can attribute a significant portion of their success to lessons learned on their quest to attain a college degree. As I reflect upon some of the exceptional leaders that I have studied over the years, it is clear that the pursuit of education is quintessential for leadership development. One of my favorite cases is that of Michelle Obama. Michelle's life story is a showcase of Black Girl Magic.

Raised on Chicago's south side, Michelle observed the potentially detrimental effects of disinvestment in the community and learned the value of educational investment first-hand as her parents instilled a love of learning and seeking educational opportunities within her and her brother early in their childhood. By the sixth grade, Michelle was labeled as gifted and completed accelerated courses in many subjects. She graduated as her class salutatorian. Her scholastic achievements and display of leadership in her class and community earned her acceptance into Princeton University, where she graduated Cum Laude.

Aware that there was more for her to accomplish, Michelle then went on to study law at Harvard Law School where she participated in demonstrations advocating for diversification of the student body and faculty by calling for the enrollment and hiring of minority students and professors. Shortly after law school, Michelle worked as a corporate attorney but decided she wanted to pursue something closer to her passion, a career in public service and the rest is history being made. Her public service career began as an assistant in the office of Chicago's then Mayor. She then went on to become the executive director for the Chicago Office of Public Allies and a dean at the University of Chicago. While serving as executive director, she was appointed vice president for Community and External Affairs for the University of Chicago Medical Center.[12]

Today, Michelle Obama is a figure of empowerment and a spokeswoman for change. During her tenure as First Lady, she focused her attention on remediating issues plaguing marginalized communities, especially health and wellness and women finding the work-life balance almost every professional struggles to find. One of her most recent endeavors includes launching the Global Girls Alliance, a program of the Obama Foundation that seeks to empower adolescent girls around the world through education.

I find Michelle Obama's story to be inspirational to say the least, but I could have highlighted many other women of color who have leveraged the opportunity to pursue post-secondary education just like Michelle. Women like Ethel Hedgeman Lyle, the founder of Alpha Kappa Alpha Sorority, Inc., the nation's first Greek-letter organization for college educated African-American women founded in

12 Biography.com Authors, "Michelle Obama Biography," April 2014. https://www.biography.com/people/michelle-obama-307592

1908. I repeat, 1908. Jane Bolin, the first Black woman to become a U.S. judge, Dr. Chien-Shiung Wu, often referred to as "The First Lady of Physics" made significant scientific contributions that disproved the law of Conservation of Parity, Raffi Freedman-Gurspan, the first openly transgender person to work as a White House staffer, Indra Nooyi, 2006 – 2018 CEO of the second largest food and beverage industry in the world, *PepsiCo*, who has earned recognition as one of the world's most influential business women, I could go on and on…and on.

When you read their bios and learn more about their professional journeys, you'll observe implementation of what my mom calls the "P5 Method: Proper Planning Prevents Poor Performance." Earning a degree is not just something that happens. It takes planning. It takes great work, but it has the potential to reap even greater rewards.

The Brown Girl's Guide to College gives you a roadmap that makes the P5 Method personal to you. *Part One: Before It All Begins* provides a step-by-step account of what you need to do before you step foot on campus. *Part Two: When You Get There* focuses on how you can maximize your potential and take advantage of opportunities once you're there and *Part Three: What's Next* gives you the information you need to set the stage for your life after-college.

Take it from me, it's better you do what you need to do and implement the P5 Method in as many ways as you can now, so you don't have to spend time backtracking later. While writing this foreword, I'm in the midst of studying for my exams to become a Certified Public Accountant (CPA). I admit that it's tough because it is not my favorite thing to do, but I know earning this certification will lead to greater opportunities for me to do one of my favorite things – helping others reach a level of financial freedom they would not have otherwise met without my assistance. The CPA is a four-part exam. To date, I've passed two exams and failed two exams. Those failures were a direct result of me making a conscious decision not to implement the "P5 Method" I mentioned earlier. I did not study accordingly. Five-minute breaks turned into hour long scrolls down my TL, listening to podcasts, going to get food, everything but continuance of my study session. So, here I am again – having to find the will and time to study for another exam and while I am super excited about being a CPA one day, there are many other things I want to do to fulfill the plan God has for me - things I could be doing in if I didn't have to study again.

As explained in *The Guide,* there will undoubtedly be times during your collegiate career when you feel like you made a mistake, when you feel like you did not plan accordingly. While you can certainly recover from almost every mistake, plan to make the right choice today to invest the time to read the *The Brown Girl's Guide to College.* Reading this guide will help you properly plan to prevent poor performance in college.

We will all have to answer thousands of questions over the course of a lifetime. Beyoncé has already posed one of the most important questions to us: "Who runs the world?" The answer: "Girls!" To be specific, girls like you. Girls like you who are ready to make major moves, take the next step to embark on what are going to be some of the best years of your lives, and join the community of college graduates around the world who look like…you.

As you prepare to work through *The BGGC,* know that you are receiving words of wisdom from women who have successfully implemented the "P5 Method" and secured their seats at the table. I've read *The Guide* multiple times and each time, even as someone with two college degrees, I find something I wish I would have known prior to graduating. Taylor, Amber, Paige, and Asia have been in your shoes and want you to plan to wear the shoes they now wear walking the walk as college graduates. Working through *the Browns Girls Guide to College* is a great place to start.

Keniece Gray

Cleveland, Ohio

Part One: Before It All Begins

Are you ready to embark on a journey that encompasses some of the best years of your life? Soon, you will transition from being a high school student to an independent college student, but do not worry. You won't be doing this alone. We have been right where you are. We were worried about our next steps after high school; we were frustrated with our parents during the application process; and we were also eager to get out and be "grown." We said all of this to say that we know exactly how you feel, and because of that, we are here to give you advice to aid in your pursuit of a college degree. Did we forget to mention that we also look like you? As women of color, we have not always had the guidance, support, or resources we needed to pursue a college degree. Therefore, we have gathered the information we learned along the way and put it here in hopes of becoming your fellow Brown Girl support sisters. We have gone through this process and are going to give you tips on what we know and what we wish we had known before we embarked on this journey.

> *"The future belongs to those who believe in the beauty of their dreams."*
> *Eleanor Roosevelt*

> *"Bearing the gifts that my ancestors gave, I am the dream and the hope of a slave" Still I Rise, Maya Angelou*

For many that are reading this book, the journey that lies ahead of you is unfamiliar. Not only to you, but to your parents and generations before you. Have you considered how amazing of an opportunity you have sitting right before you? For many of us, our parents did not complete college. Some of us have grandparents that may not have finished high school; but here you are thinking about college. You are seeking out opportunities to educate yourself on the process with the hope that you will get into college and unlock the doors to your future. Don't fret, don't worry, and don't stress because we've got

> *There is a time and season for everything.*

your back!

So, you may be thinking about where you should begin when approaching the whole college application process. Thankfully, you are preparing to go to college during the twenty-first century. You have access to resources and tools that were not available to many women of color that went before you. Although these resources are truly amazing, they can be overwhelming. Before you get nose-deep in Google searches, you should really take some time to think about what you are looking for.

Timeline

There is a time and season for everything. You should strive to use our outline as a framework for your application process. Of course, some portions of the process can be moved around, but the general framework should help you prepare for a less stressful application process. From our experience, minority applicants do not know all of the preparation that goes in to having a strong college application. This causes some minority applicants to not complete the requirements in optimal time. We want to help make sure that you are both aware of the timeline and are timely with submissions.

College Prep In High School Timeline:

Freshman Year:

- Meet with your high school guidance counselor to develop a plan for a successful and timely high school graduation.
- Ensure you have the highest Grade Point Average (GPA) possible. You want to start off strong.
- Take a career assessment test.
- Begin exploring different career/education paths.
- Join and actively participate in extracurricular activities.
- Begin serving your community through local community service organizations.
- Research summer enrichment organizations that will either help prepare you for college or expose you to potential careers.
- Begin researching and applying for scholarships.
- Start gathering PSAT, ACT, SAT study materials.
- Complete a summer internship or enrichment program the summer following your freshman year.

Sophomore Year:

- Continue to excel in your courses.
- Study for and take the PLAN and PSAT.
- Take a career assessment test.
- Join and actively participate in extracurricular activities.
- Continue exploring careers and the education requirements for those careers.
- Continue applying for scholarships
- Begin college visits.
- Continue doing community service.
- Complete a summer internship or enrichment program the summer following your sophomore year.

Junior Year:

- Ensure that you are on track to graduate.
- Ask for letters of recommendation from your teachers, mentors and community leaders.
- Start to think about your personal statement.
- Continue applying for scholarships.
- Take ACT/SAT, and retake if needed.
- Gather financial information for FAFSA.
- Visit colleges.
- Complete a summer internship or enrichment program the summer following your junior year.

Senior Year:

May-July before Senior year starts

- Go on college visits.
- Continue applying for scholarships.
- Begin gathering college application materials.

August- December

- Start and complete college applications.
- Continue visiting colleges.
- Continue applying for scholarships.

January- March

- Await college acceptances.
- Visit colleges with the goal of your visit helping you narrow your choices.

Summer Enrichment programs are programs that help you further your education or extra-curricular interests outside of your regular high school. Some summer enrichment programs occur in cities across the world. The benefit of attending a summer enrichment program is that you form meaningful relationships with the other participants, you further your knowledge and experience in a particular subject matter and you get exposed to educational settings outside of your normal environment.

FAFSA Applications open in October. Complete your FAFSA in October of your senior year of high school.

Completing your college visits during summer allows you to visit colleges when your schedule is a bit more flexible. On the other hand, visiting colleges while you are in school will allow for you to see the university while courses are in session. Though this may cause you to miss class, most schools will allow for those absences to be excused. Make sure to check with your guidance counselor for your school's policy on attendance and college visits!

The Common App opens August 1 each year. Gather all your application materials and be prepared to apply as soon as applications open.

- Continue to apply for scholarships.
- Work with your narrowed list to finalize your financial aid *BEFORE* paying your seat deposit.

As you can see applying for scholarships is a continuous activity. Scholarship deadlines approach each month of the year. You should always be searching and applying for scholarships throughout the year.

April

- Choose a college.
- Finalize your financial aid.
- Continue to apply for scholarships.
- Pay your seat deposit.

May-June

- Celebrate your high school graduation!
- Continue to apply for scholarships.
- Complete a summer internship or enrichment program before leaving for college.

Brown girls, we have developed a five-step process that encompasses all the steps necessary to guide you through the college application and the college selection process. We suggest that you read through the entire section, then go back and begin each step. Doing it this way makes sure that you have general familiarity with all that is involved in the process. Throughout this process you will be creating several documents. We recommend that you create a folder on a computer to hold all of these documents. You can use a thumb drive, an online cloud service or a computer to save your documents. Whatever you use, make sure that you have things saved in a backup location such as an external hard drive. Technology is a beautiful resource, but it sometimes crashes!

STEP ONE: The Application Process (Prepare for Success)

Research & Create Your Application Checklist

"I am deliberate and afraid of nothing." Audrey Lorde

You can start researching schools as early as your freshman year of high school! If you start researching early you will need to update all factual information in your spreadsheet the summer

---

Compiling your list this way helps you save time during this phase of the application process. You will soon learn that this task will take a lot of time. Plan to work on your spreadsheet a little bit each day.

Settle your fear by preparing for what is to come. The first step is to research schools. There are many ways you can do this, but we recommend that you start with a general search. People choose their school based on location, degrees offered, class sizes, whether it's private or public, price, and scholarship funds. As you research, you will find schools with things that you like, and things you do not like. Use the exercise that you completed above to help guide your research. In a spreadsheet, begin to make a list of all of the schools that spark your interest. We suggest that you make a "checklist." Your checklist will have the school name, location, cost of attendance, size and the application process. This will help you down the road because there is no way that you will remember all of this critical information for each school. By the end of Part I, you should have a complete and lengthy list of colleges and universities! Make sure to visit our resources section in the back of the book for a sample spreadsheet template.

Since I was in high school, I always loved biology and wanted to be a doctor. When I was looking for schools, I put my focus on institutions that had good science programs and would adequately prepare me to get into medical school. -Paige J.

I wanted small class sizes. Usually, private liberal-arts colleges are known for having smaller class sizes than large state-funded, public colleges. Out of that list, I tried to find schools that were well- known for my intended major. -Taylor F.

The institution I chose to attend had a goal of making sure that every student at the institution had at least one global experience while they were in school. Before attending college, I had never been abroad. Therefore, this was one of my personal goals for college and was a major factor in choosing the school I attended. It worked out because I was able to go one three different funded trips abroad. -Asia P.

I chose a private, smaller school because I wanted to have more one-on-one time with my professors. I work better in smaller settings and wanted to ensure that I could excel in class. -Amber C.

Each sub-heading in "The Requirements" section should be a heading in your spreadsheet checklist.

Your goal should be to receive an acceptance letter AND scholarships.

Things To Consider When Looking At Schools

Degree Programs
Size
Location
Safety
Health
Your Values
Opportunities for Study Abroad
Clubs & Organizations
Public/Private

The Requirements

Admissions Tests

Let's be real, no one likes standardized tests. Though most don't like them, they are a necessary to gain college acceptance. While we will not spend a lot of time on standardized test prep, we will spend some time with a general discussion on tests. We are sure you have heard of the ACT and SAT by now. But in case you have not, the ACT and SAT are required standardized tests for any person seeking college admission. The test is used as measurement tool by colleges to help determine your ability to handle the rigors of college. While these tests are critical, most colleges take a holistic approach when evaluating test scores. What that means is that your score is only *one* factor in determining your acceptance. Although your scores are one factor in your application, we would like to note that scoring above average should be the goal. Think about it like this, colleges and universities receive thousands of applications each year. Those with strong applications will be more likely to receive an acceptance letter and scholarship offer. The weaker your application is, the weaker your chance is for acceptance; and scholarship offers diminish.

Further, your admission test scores will help you attain the second part of your goal: scholarships. Many (but not all) scholarships are awarded as a result of your admission test scores. Depending on the school, certain institutions will allow you to qualify for certain merit-based scholarships in-state and nationally. Therefore, it is imperative that you do your best.

In order to get some early practice for the ACT and SAT, you can take the PSAT or the PLAN. Usually, the PSAT is taken during your sophomore or junior year of high school. But since you are going to be an awesome Brown Girl scholar, you should aim to take it your sophomore year of high school. If you score well on the PSAT, you can qualify for National Merit Scholarships!

So, how do you excel on your admissions tests? We each decided to take a different path during the process. It is important to remember that you are a unique individual so your approach to acing your admission tests should match your learning style. Though you will take an individual approach for studying, there are two things that will remain the same. No matter what, you will have to study and the deadlines will remain the same. Start preparing the summer before your sophomore year of high school. Doing this ensures that you have enough time to study and meet all of your deadlines. Also, during your sophomore year, you will take the courses needed to do well on the test. Once those courses are completed, you will know most of what you will see on the test.

National Merit Scholarships are scholarships given as a part of a United States Academic competition. The first step in the academic competition is acing the PSAT. Make sure to check out our resources section for more information about National Merit Scholarships!

Study means investing time and money into your success. Make sure to take advantage of all resources that exist. (blogs, youtube, tutors and handbooks). "One thing that really helped me was sitting for timed practice tests. In this way, you mimic what the true test conditions and timing will be like." -Paige Jones

---

Begin preparing for your admission test the summer before your sophomore year. Then take your test by the end of your sophomore year.

Make sure to check out our resources section for more information on fee waivers!

You can also get your test answers and test questions back from the ACT. They will provide you with information on how they scored your test and all of the correct answers. It's called Test Information Release. For the SAT it is called the Answer Verification Services. This can help you figure out why you pick certain answers and what sections you need to improve on.

If your school does not offer test prep sessions, some churches and nonprofits have ACT/SAT Prep classes for free!

Most important, you do not want to wait to take your admission tests because it takes time to get your scores back. Plus, there is a chance that you may need to retake the test; and your best test score is necessary to complete your college application. At the latest, have your test completed by August of your senior year. Keep in mind that all of these standardized tests, including the ACT and SAT cost money. That's right! You might have to sacrifice a manicure, or two to pay for it! Although applying to college will cost you some money, most high schools offer at least one free ACT test date, and other financial resources. Visit your school counselor's office to get more information on additional financial assistance that may be available in your area.

Because we have been where you are, we want to make sure that we are honest with you. Taking a standardized test will be difficult, but it is not impossible. We want you to know that not one of us took the test just one time. It took us a couple of times to get it right, and there is nothing wrong with that. If you find yourself in a situation where you are unable to attain the score that you want, reach out to your guidance counselor to inquire about what support systems your school has in place to help with test prep. And if you still find yourself having trouble, remember that your standardized tests are still only ONE area that you will be evaluated on during the admissions process. Just do YOUR best every time you take your test!

The Application

You will have to apply to each college that you are interested in attending. To aid in streamlining the process there are services like "The Common Application," "The Common Black Application" and "Quest." These services allow you to apply to more than one institution at once. This cuts down on time and helps streamline the process. Depending on the institution, there will be additional information and essays required. Take advantage of the streamlined serves and save time where you can, but pay very close attention to individualized requirements.

Visit our resources section to see a list of application streamlining services.

Your personal statement is a short piece of writing about you purposed to bring your application to life. Make sure to visit our resources section for more information on personal statements

---

"Your life story is unique. You have unique perspectives, a unique personality, and unique experiences that colleges want to know about." -Asia Payne

---

When writing, find something that will grab your reader's attention from the beginning.

When writing your personal statement heavy editing is a must which is why we suggest that you begin writing early. You should have several people look over your writing prior to turning it in. When you are finished writing, read it out loud to yourself, then have someone else read it to ensure that it says exactly what you want it to say.

Personal Statement

Your personal statement is a short piece of writing about you purposed to bring your application to life. Cranking out a personal statement can seem daunting but think of it as an opportunity for you to stand out. Your life story is unique. You have unique perspectives, a unique personality, and unique experiences that colleges want to know about. A common mistake that people make when writing their personal statement is just listing off things that they have accomplished in life. This is a huge mistake! Listing off accomplishes restates everything that admissions would already know about you from reading your application or reviewing your resume. Your personal statement should bring the content of your application to life.

The goal for your personal statement is to grab the reader's attention in the first sentence or paragraph with an anecdote or story that shares an interesting experience from your past. Then share some of the activities you did during high school, including community service, sports, or any other extracurriculars and how they have shaped you into the best college applicant. Connect all of that together in a way that will keep your readers attention throughout. The biggest piece of advice that we want to give is that you should be authentic in whatever you write. Be you! Last, but not least, you should plan on writing your personal statement the summer before you apply to college. Make sure you check our resources section for a sample personal statement.

Ask for your letters of recommendation early! Check our resources section for a sample email request template.

DO NOT ask family members for letters of recommendation! This is frowned upon! Coaches, Volunteer Coordinators, Sponsors of Organizations you are involved in, are a great recommenders. Also, a teacher you received an excellent grade in or a class that you worked very hard to achieve the grade you received, and the teacher recognizes this are great examples of people you should ask for letters of recommendation.

Your brag sheet is usually comprised of the important activities you participate in and the qualities about yourself that you want your recommender to highlight in your recommendation letter. See our resources section for an example of a brag sheet.

A resume lists all of your leadership positions, volunteer activities, grade point average, and jobs. Visit the resources section for a sample resume.

Recommendation Letters

"Recommendation Letters" or "Letters of Recommendation" are letters written by people who know you and can attest to your academic excellence, commitment to a particular initiative or your demonstrated work ethic. "Recommenders" is the term used for the people who consent to writing you a letter of recommendation. The key to securing your recommenders is to ask early! It is best to request recommendation letters from a teacher immediately after you finish their course (because you don't want them to forget specifics about you) or by the spring semester of your junior year of high school. Timing is critical. If you wait until the fall semester of your senior year, you will be competing with other students who are seeking a letter as well. The earlier you request the letter, the better.

Remember, you want to have "favorable" and "strong" letters. When writing to your potential recommenders, make sure to specifically ask if they are able to write a strong *and* favorable letter. You may discover that someone who is writing a recommendation for you does not know you as well as you perceived, which means their recommendation will not be strong. For example, although you may be heavily involved in a student organization at school, the advisor of the organization may not know you that well if you all have never had a sit-down conversation.

Choose people who know you well, who can confirm their ability to give you a strong and favorable recommendation and can talk about how fabulous of a scholar, student, and person you are.

Some of the people writing your recommendations will want you to provide additional information about yourself to help them write your letter. To get that additional information, they might ask for personal statements, a brag sheet, or a resume, So, have copies available for them when you ask them to write your letter.

Deadlines

Set calendar reminders on your cell phone to help remind you of any upcoming deadlines.

Make sure to stay on top of deadlines. Each college has different application deadlines. We suggest that you complete all of your applications by November 1st of your senior year. This is usually the deadline for early acceptance and gives you a better chance at obtaining scholarship money. Add each college deadline to your spreadsheet. You don't want to turn in an application late. Most colleges will not consider late applications since they are already receiving thousands of other applications.

STEP TWO:
Scholarships, Loans & Financial Aid

Research & Apply for Scholarships and Financial Aid

Did you know that you can apply for scholarships way before your senior year of high school? Visit our resources section to find out more information.

Money, money, money! When thinking about money for college, there are roughly six streams that money for college can flow from. Money can come from institutional aid, outside scholarships, grants, loans, parents/family and YOU! Your goal should be to get as much institutional aid, outside aid and grants as possible. Doing that reduces the amount of help you will need to secure from other resources. The first step to attaining that goal is to research what opportunities are available to you. You should apply for scholarships throughout your high school career. The key lesson to learn from this is that it is never too early to begin applying for outside scholarships. Scholarship deadlines occur year-round. There are so many scholarships in the world that there are some that are just easier to receive because less people apply.

Stream 1: FAFSA

Completing the FAFSA is the first step to attaining aid for college. Everyone is required to fill out the FAFSA. It helps colleges know how much Federal Aid you qualify for, and how much aid you will need based on how much money your family earns annually. The Federal Government figures out how much aid you qualify for based on a variety of factors. They look at your family size, your family's gross annual income, your family's tax returns and so much more. To complete the FAFSA you will need your parent or guardian's financial information (including their most recent tax returns) when completing your FAFSA.

Stream 2: Institutional Aid

Institutional Aid is the aid that you receive from each institution that you apply to. The institutional aid that you receive applies to that particular institution. Institutional Aid is granted based on your academic excellence, extra-curricular involvement, geographic location and career interests. In order to see what institutional aid is available you should look at the "Financial Aid" section on each college's admissions page. Most schools include a list of scholarships available and a short description about who that scholarship is typically awarded to. Eligibility for institutional aid is sometimes evaluated with your admissions application. Other times, institutional aid will require a separate application process.

Stream 3: Outside Scholarships

Outside scholarships are scholarships that are available outside of the individual institutions. These scholarships are endless. Outside scholarships require a separate application for each scholarship that you are applying to. Sometimes these applications require essays and letters of recommendations. There are several scholarship search engines that list scholarships. Make sure to visit the resources section for common outside scholarship search engines.

Stream 4: Grants

Grants are similar to outside scholarships. There are many sources for grants. Some grants like the Pell Grant are awarded by the Federal Government based off of information that you provided in your FAFSA. Other grants are available through companies and non-profit organizations. Grants that are not awarded through FAFSA require a separate application.

Stream 5: Loans

Up until this point we have provided information on avenues that will not require repayment. Loans are a stream that require repayment. You can receive loans for your education through the federal government, banks, and external education loan providers. An in-depth break down on the different types of loans that are available in the resources section. Make sure to review that section if you find yourself needing loans to cover your balance.

Stream 6: Parents/Family

Your parents or family may be a source to help pay for your college education. If you get down this low in our stream of income chart you should have a discussion with your parents about where you stand with money for college. Having this conversation early in the process is so important!

Stream 7: You

You, yes you are the last stream of income. You are your last resource. For some applicants, they know from the beginning that they will be responsible for any balance that is not covered by streams one through four. You paying your balance should be your last resort.

STEP THREE: You've applied. Now what?

Step Two, Check! You've applied, now what? You may think that it's all done now. You may think there is nothing else that you can do until you find out whether you have been accepted into a particular school. While you could sit around and wait on an acceptance letter, a better use of your time would be to engage with the schools that you have applied, apply for scholarships and participate in extracurricular programs.

Your engagement with colleges and universities does not end when you submit your application. One of the key moments in the college application process is continuing to engage with the universities that you have chosen to apply to. Interestingly enough, some of the opportunities to engage with universities will come straight from the university, hand-crafted to show you the most glorious aspects that the university has to offer. Others however will be created by you. No matter what path you take, it is important that you continue to engage with the schools.

It is critical for you to engage with colleges and universities BEFORE *and* AFTER you apply for admission. Doing this has a reciprocal benefit for both you and the institution. Remember, it should be your goal to receive a letter of acceptance from the college of your choice AND to receive a generous financial aid award from the university. In our experience, your chances of meeting that goal are higher when you take the dedicated effort of engaging with colleges and universities. Why? Colleges want to know that you are genuinely interested in attending their school. Today, with the further development of streamlined undergraduate application processes it becomes easier for prospective students to apply to multiple colleges at once. When you take the next steps like visiting the university, setting up meetings with the professors, attending admissions sponsored events, and observing classes, you are showing the university that you are seriously interested in attending the school. Engaging with the university also helps you determine very early in the process whether or not that school will be a good fit for you. In our new technology age, it is easy to get caught up with only looking at things online. Now, college websites can give you 3-D virtual tours of campuses. Those colleges create their own websites in an effort to attract prospective students, so naturally, they will never showcase their weaknesses. This is why it is helpful to talk to current students. In our resources section, we have included an important chart that will be valuable in helping you engage with colleges.

When I was applying to college, I attended about three different college fairs where I could engage with representatives from various colleges and universities. I also visited most of the colleges I applied to through scheduled visit days. Some schools allowed me to shadow a student for the day. Others had informational sessions, followed by a tour of the campus. These campus visit days ultimately helped me decide on which school I wanted to attend. You want to feel comfortable on the campus and be able to picture yourself there. Talk to the students and ask them detailed questions about their personal experiences at the school because usually they will give you an honest answer. On that note, make sure you ask a student that isn't giving the tour. Once I was accepted to college, I attended the revisit day for the school I matriculated into. This was an up and close experience in which I stayed in one of the residence halls of the school, talked to students, met with professors from different departments, and immersed myself in the culture of the campus. Also, I was able to pay my enrollment deposit to officially attend. -Asia Payne

---

Before visiting CBU, I talked with people who I knew attended. I wanted a perspective that didn't come from people giving tours, but who would be honest about their experience. I heard about good and bad things, which helped me make decision to visit the campus and participate in events that the school offered for prospective students. -Amber Campbell

---

"Your chances of meeting that goal are higher when you take the dedicated effort of engaging with colleges and universities." -Taylor Flake

Engaging with Colleges & Universities

College visits are essential to the college application process. By deciding to visit a college, you are showing the university your interest in their particular program, and you are proving that you are looking at that college with the intent of finding out whether it is a good fit for you. It is important that you realize very early on that there are *many* great schools. There will be schools that have exactly what you want, and there will be schools that have less of what you want. However, it is important that you find the school that is perfect for *you*. And *you* are the only person that can determine that. To help illustrate the point we are trying to make, we want to share our experiences concerning college visits. What you will see is that each story is unique. Not only did our visits help us engage with the college but they also helped with the decision-making process, which will be discussed in Step Four.

"I knew that I preferred to go away from home for college because I just always knew that I wanted to explore other parts of the United States. I was looking forward to meeting new people, learning about new cultures, and figuring myself out without the influence of my familiar surroundings. I fell in love with the institution I chose to attend the moment I stepped onto the campus. I literally felt so comfortable and at home when talking to the faculty and professors. I knew that I would be at an institution that would support me in the sciences, as this was what I wanted to go into. I also knew that there was no limit to what I could achieve because this was the culture that the institution cultivated.-Asia"

"I wasn't interested in staying home for college. Because of this, I wasn't really excited about touring schools that were in my hometown. I would go and think "this is okay, but it's not what I want." I visited schools, virtually and in person, and the school I felt most connected to was CBU. At the time I thought my dream school would be in Nashville, but when I visited, the school didn't feel welcoming. That was definitely a damper. Once I visited CBU, I could actually picture myself there. I spoke with professors who were extremely nice and helpful. I spoke with students who gave their honest opinions, and overall I realized it was right where I needed to be. My high school guidance counselor always said that "it's better to be a big fish in a little pond, than a small fish in a big pond." At the time, I thought she was saying that I couldn't thrive at a big school. But I soon realized that she meant "go where I could make the greatest impact." And at CBU, I was able to do just that! -Amber"

"I visited three colleges during my senior year. The first was gorgeous and the curriculum seemed to be what I needed to go into medicine. It was definitely ranked high on my list. The second one was was ok, but for some reason it didn't really stand out to me. The last one I visited was Xavier and I absolutely LOVED my experience. The number of African-Americans who were getting into medical school was astounding. Visiting my top choices definitely made choosing much easier and gave me a small insight to how my college experience would be. -Paige"

"Thinking back on my application process, I remember applying to over twenty schools. Some were big, some were small, some had many majors to choose from and others had a narrower selection. I remember getting the same advice that we are giving to you, "find the school that is right for YOU." I thought I understood what it meant, but I really did not. To be completely transparent, I ended up choosing to attend a small, private Catholic school in my hometown, that doubles as the same university that my mom attended to obtain her master's degree. Don't get me wrong, she loved the school. I often remember her coming home and raving about how much I would like the school and how I should consider attending when it's time for me to go to college. But like most high schoolers, I really wasn't trying to hear anything she had to say. I remember applying, getting a scholarship interview and really not wanting to go. I begged my mom to let me skip the tour and breakfast that the university scheduled before the actual interview. My excuse was "What do I need a tour of the school for? The campus is so small I can throw a rock from one side and it will land on the other." As you would expect, I was still forced to go on the tour.

Moral of the story is, when I went on the tour, this Brown Girl fell in love. The campus was beautiful, and it truly felt like home. What made the visit even better was that I was interviewed by an alum and a current professor. While being interviewed by the alum, I learned how her experience during undergrad at that particular university was truly life changing. For some reason that helped me. During my second interview with the professor, I remember him starting the interview by asking me a really basic question about the university's foundation and mission. Of course, I did not know the answer to the question, but he kindly explained the university's mission which began to shed light on their commitment to education, students, and service. I really value companies, organizations and universities that are intentional about integrating their mission into everything that they do. So, naturally, that was the deciding factor for me. Out of all of the schools I applied to and visited, this was the only one that mentioned its mission and explained how it was integrated into the fabric of the school.

I like to tell that story because it can give applicants just a glimpse into the many things that you can learn when you decide to visit a school. Most colleges and universities that know what they are doing will make sure that you have the chance to sit in on a class, talk to a current student and talk to a current professor when you visit. If you are attending a special event that is being hosted by the admissions department, you may be able to talk to alum. Truthfully, sitting in on a class, talking to a current student (preferably in the discipline that you plan to study), talking with a current professor and speaking with an alumnus are major moments to help you see what the school is all about. If you have this opportunity, soak it all in.

Choose a school based on what YOU value! Make a list of what you like and dislike before making your visit! Self-Awareness during this stage of the application process is critical.

So, whether you decide to make the visit before you receive your acceptance letter or after you are accepted, college visits are critical in aiding in the decision-making process. You are the only person that knows you. You know what you like, you know what you dislike. Take a moment and think about what you like and what you dislike. What are things that you value? What things can you just not stand? Keep these things in mind during the decision-making process. Your self-awareness can sometimes be the best decision maker for you. For me, knowing what I valued helped me make my decision, and it can help you too. Finally, it is important to note that there are some things you should pay close attention to or ask about on your visit. -Taylor"

College is much different in high school. When contacting professors verbally and in writing make sure to use the appropriate title. In college "Ms. Mrs. and Mr." are no longer used. Instead use Professor, or Dr.

Alumni are individuals who graduated from the college or university

---

Your advisors are usually assigned to you and are a part of your major's department. It's best to meet with your advisors early to understand how they will be advising you. Some will expect you to come in with specific questions, know which classes you want to take and be thorough with their time. Some will be more laid back; will help you create your schedule and will be willing to talk with you for hours.

I shadowed a student for a day, and I was able to attend classes with her like an actual student. I ate lunch with her and met some of her classmates. It was a great way to see the structure of the classes and to get student perspectives.
-Asia

Professors, Current Students & Alumni

Talking to professors, current students and alumni are great while on college visits. The reality is, depending on when you decide to visit, you may not be able to get everything in that you would like to while you are on the campus. But you can still engage with the professors, current students and alumni after you leave. Let's discuss the important roles the professors, current students and alumni each play with respect to their college/university. Our resources section and workbook outlines specific conversation starters that you can use as a guide when you begin engaging with people of these groups.

After you enroll and begin classes at a university, your professors are the people that you will see on a consistent basis, whether it is in class, at extra-curricular organization meetings, at work study, or in advising meetings. They are the people that you will develop a relationship with that will hopefully extend beyond your college journey. Since you will spend a lot of time with your professors during the course of your academic journey, we find it helpful to try to engage with them before you attend the university. When you meet with professors, you should try to talk to them about their interests as well as their publications outside of the classroom. It is also important to ask about their advising style because your advisors play an important role in helping you pair your coursework with your post-graduation goals. Knowing that the professors have advised students that are working in the area that you want to work in is helpful because you know you will at least have a reliable resource during your journey through college.

Students are the lifelines of universities. Without students, universities would likely not exist. Thus, it is important that you talk to as many students as possible. You should talk to students in your desired major, outside of your major, organization leaders and regular students. Each individual experience is valuable, and it can give you a good idea of those that you will be around during your tenure. One way to hear from students is to ask to shadow a student. During this process, you will have the chance to spend a day with students, go to their classes, have lunch with them, go to their extracurricular activities and so-forth.

When it comes to engaging with alumni, you should focus on asking about how their experience during undergrad aided in their professional success today. You should ask about what classes and professors they found helpful both during their journey through undergrad and today in their fields.

STEP FOUR: Making the Decision

There is no perfect decision in choosing a college. Go with what feels right, and what school you feel you will thrive. After all, college is what YOU make of it. You can be successful wherever you go!

Congrats Brown girl! You have now entered decision-making territory! Whether it's one, or two, or ten, every acceptance is a reason for you to be proud of yourself and your accomplishments. Step Four is aimed at giving you the information you need to help you make an informed decision. This is truly a big decision, so you need to make sure you are making an informed one.

Before we dive into helping you make that informed decision, we need to talk about what a lot of people hate talking about. Rejection. It happens to all of us. Waitlisted? That happened to us too. Remember how we said we are here for you? Keep reading and we will offer some strategies that will help you navigate that experience.

Waitlisted/Rejected: What to do when the decision has been made for you.

If you are waitlisted or rejected from a school, do not get discouraged. Most schools have particular quotas that they have to fill, and even if you meet all the criteria, you may not get accepted. If you are waitlisted for a school, this means that the school has reached their number of acceptances for that term. The waitlist is for qualified candidates who will be contacted for acceptance if some of the students already accepted decide to not attend that school. If you are waitlisted, you will be notified of your application status. After all of the students accept or deny admission, the school will go through the waitlist and call the students on the list. If you are at the top of the list, you will be one of the first people called. If you are at the bottom, you may or may not receive a call immediately. A waitlist can go either way and does not guarantee admission. One strategy to help move you from the waitlist to admission is to send a letter of continued interest. We have included a sample in our resources section.

A rejection does not mean that you are not worthy of attending that school, or that you won't get accepted anywhere else.

"Remain focused on the overall goal of starting college. One closed door means there are plenty more that are open for you."

If you are rejected from a school, do not let that discourage you from furthering your education. That school will miss out on the presence of really awesome Brown Girl on their campus. A rejection does not mean that you are not worthy of attending that school, or that you won't get accepted anywhere else. It simply means that the school may not be meant for you. Rejection happens to almost everyone that applies to college, so you will not be the only person that experiences it. It is always good to have backup schools that are just as good and are of the same quality and caliber that you would like to further your career at as well. Attending your second or third school of choice is just as great as attending your first. Remain focused on the overall goal of starting college. One closed door means there are plenty more that are open for you.

Narrowing it Down

You have your acceptances and you are trying to narrow down where you will attend. You should remember that no college is the same. There are various factors that change depending on the institution. To help you narrow your list, we have included broad information and discussions about different aspects of college. These discussions should provide you with more information to help you narrow your options.

Types of Colleges

So let's start with the type of college. There are many categories to consider (PWI, HBCU, Public, Private, Religious, Liberal Arts, etc.). But for now, let's focus on the big ones. We would like to note that there are advantages and disadvantages that come with attending any college. In the section below, we aim to provide you with information that will help shape your understanding about the different types of universities that exist.

PWI

A PWI or a Predominately White Institution, is a category that fits a large percentage of the colleges in the United States. Usually, minorities make up about 5-20 percent of the entire student body depending on the school. Below are a few facts that we think would help inform you about Predominantly White Institutions.

Predominantly White Institutions:

- Have an environment that is similar to the workforce or corporate world.
- Often have more money and resources. The evidence of the money and resources can be seen in the type of facilities, the extent of technology in the classrooms, and the level of institutional scholarships offered.
- Have a diverse alumni networking pool.

HBCU

So now, "HBCU", or Historically Black College (or) University. These institutions were established to give African Americans a chance to receive a college degree at a time when other colleges wouldn't allow African Americans to pursue post-secondary education. Their influence, relevance, and values are still important today. Many students decide to attend an HBCU because they went to a predominantly white high school and want to be more engrossed with their own culture. Others attend because of their family legacy (their parents and grandparents attended the same school), or because many HBCUs are generous with institutional scholarships.

Historically Black Institutions:

- Have a student population and successful alumni that look more like you.
- Have a comfortable yet challenging environment that pushes and encourages you.

- Foster an atmosphere that represents black culture. This can help you define your identity and what you represent.

Size

Another thing to consider is the size of the campus. We know what you're thinking. Girl, I'm just out here trying to get an education, why should size matter? Just hear us out on this. Size is actually quite important, especially depending on your learning style. For example, a large school comprised of about 10,000+ people, would mean bigger classes with lectures in huge rooms. When you need one-on-one assistance from your professor during office hours, your professor may be more difficult to access due to large class sizes. Imagine trying to share that one teacher with 99+ other people. It also makes it a tad bit harder to form a relationship with your professors for letters of recommendation and such. On the other hand, a bigger campus can also benefit you as well. You may have a diverse population that you can meet and learn from.

So, what about a small school? Smaller schools generally mean smaller classes, and more time with your professors. If you get anxiety with larger crowds or you prefer more intimate settings, a smaller school may be best for you.

State vs Private

Next on the list is state versus private, which almost runs hand in hand with the large versus small school comparison. State schools, which tend to be on the larger side, are called such because they receive funding from the state. This is great because tuition is generally cheaper, but it can also make it harder to be awarded institutional aid. State schools tend to accept more students from their state (so they can continue being funded.) For example, if you are from Florida trying to attend a school in California, it may be more difficult to gain acceptance. State schools also make out-of-state residents pay a higher amount in tuition, which can be anywhere from $5,000 to $30,000 more compared to in state tuition.

Private schools tend to have higher tuition and are usually on the smaller side (but can be huge too; think NYU). They are more likely to give scholarships since they have a higher rate of tuition, and everyone is charged the same amount for tuition. They really do not care where you are from, but they do tend to focus on diversifying their campus.

As a senior in high school, I knew I wanted to attend law school after college. When I went to college, the program my advisor thought best fit me was a major in History and a minor in Political Science. For the most part, I've never really liked History, so I thought this was going to be a struggle. I started school and realized that being a History major wasn't going to be as bad. However, I did change to Psychology major after my first year. I liked those classes better but returned to History when I realized I might have to stay in school longer to finish the Psych major. Needless to say, once I was able to take interesting History classes, I started to enjoy my major. Choose your major wisely, and if you want to change, make sure it's the best decision for you! -Amber

Programs of Study

We want to preface this discussion about programs of study by first letting you know that it is okay not to know exactly what you want to do or what you want to study when you get to college. If you do not know what career you want to pursue, then you should look for a university that has programming to help undergraduates explore different options. On the other hand, if you do know what career you want to pursue, you need to make sure that the school actually offers what you want to study. When you make the choice to attend a school that does not offer the program of study that you want, then you may be setting yourself up for problems or frustration in the future. When thinking about universities, think about what the school is known for. If you want to be successful in the arts, go to a school that is known for its specialization in the arts. Of course, you can make a way if you decide to attend a school that does not offer your program of study; but if you can on the front end, make the choice that will help you reach your goals.

In the event that you find the perfect university, but they do not offer what you want to study, you have two options. First, you could either choose a major that is close to what you want to study and supplement it with a minor. Doing this may not seem like the perfect option, but it does get you a little closer to what you want to do. If you choose to do this, you should take some time to look at the degree and minor requirements for the program you plan to choose. When looking at the courses, ask yourself: Do they seem interesting? Will the courses help you prepare for what you ultimately want to do in life? If not, here's another option. More schools are beginning to offer interdisciplinary programs that allow you to "create your own major."

These interdisciplinary programs vary depending on the school that you choose to attend, but this option does exist. If it seems like this is something you might need to do to meet your needs, I suggest you make that known to your admissions counselor. Ask for their guidance in finding the appropriate person at the university that will be able to help offer more information on your university's offerings.

Types of Degrees

Everyone knows that going to college and graduating means that they earn a college degree, but did you know that there are a variety of degrees that you can choose from? We are going to discuss what those degrees are and how to know which one(s) are right for you.

Community Colleges are two-year junior colleges that provide affordable post-secondary education. Successful completion of a degree program at a community college will result in you receiving an associate's degree or some type of certificate. Often, students use community colleges as an avenue to a four-year institution. For example, some complete two years at a community college then transfer to a four-year school using the credits earned at their respective community college.

1. Associate Degree- This degree is earned after two years of schooling and is more widely available at community colleges. After you earn this degree you can decide to enter the workforce or attend a four-year college and earn you bachelor's degree. Many students take this route if they are not sure what they want to do or just to take advantage of community colleges being free or low cost.

2. Bachelor's Degree- This degree is earned after four years of study at a four-year college or university. These degrees are major specific (biology, history, etc.) and are awarded in broad categories. For example, degree programs in the school of science are awarded a Bachelor of Science Degree, degree programs like English, History, and art are awarded Bachelor of Arts degrees. The requirements for each vary at each school.

3. Dual and Joint Degree- Dual Degree programs allow you to work on two degrees at once. Joint Degree Programs allow you to work on a lower level degree and a professional or graduate level degree simultaneously. Often in the engineering world there is a dual degree of Electrical Engineering and Computer Science offered. Students enrolled in that sort of degree program have the opportunity to earn two bachelor's degrees in 4-5 years. Please keep in mind that the length of time for the degree program often depends on the school.

Joint degrees are similar. The main difference is that you would enter professional school at some point in your undergraduate career, usually the third or fourth year. Then when you graduate, you have your undergraduate and professional degrees under your belt. Some undergraduate institutions with ties to medical schools and pharmacy schools offer this option.

4. Certificates- If you want to take just a few credit hours so that you can apply for a specific job or get specialized training, a certificate is also an option. These are for people who just want to certify in a certain class or subject. Certificates are not degrees but they are a good way to gain specialized knowledge and valuable credentials. When thinking about certificate programs, make sure to research different programs to determine the limitations and benefits of taking this route.

Location

Location, location, location. Yes, it matters. Whether you are a small-town girl wanting to move to a big city, or from a big city and want a more intimate location, the most important thing to keep in mind is thinking about safety. Your safety should be your number one priority when looking for a city to live in for four years. Location is something else that you will be able to learn more about when you visit a school. Also, if you have something that you like to do in your free time, like playing music or dancing, look for opportunities the school and city offers to nurture that interest when you take your college visit. You do not want to be miserable for four years, and you don't have to be.

Class sizes

What high school you attended will likely influence what you expect your collegiate class sizes to be like. but class sizes could truly range from 10-300 depending on where you go to school. You may not think that this is a big issue but depending on your learning style and what you are used to, it could pose an issue for you when you begin college. It is important that you do some research to find out two important things about class sizes. You should first find out what the student to faculty ratio is. The student to faculty ratio will help you determine how many students there are in comparison to faculty. Additionally, you should ask to find out what the average class size is for first year students. This is important because some schools like to arrange for the first-year general education courses to be seminar style with many students in one

The student to faculty ratio is the number of students per faculty in the classroom. The smaller this ratio, the smaller the class sizes usually.

The average class size is the average number of students in a class.

The first year in college is critical for success. Knowing the average class size for first year students will give you a great glimpse into what your classroom experience will be like.

room. It truly just depends on what works best for you. If you have the potential to be easily distracted in large groups, then this is important information to know before you decide to attend the college. One way to figure this out is to ask admissions to allow you to sit in on a first-year class that you are interested in. That will give you the chance to observe their class sizes to help determine whether or not it is a good fit for you.

The Money

Now, for a very important question. How are you going to pay for college? College tuition continues to rise, and no one wants to take out loans, no matter how small. Figuring out where you stand financially will play a critical role in helping you narrow down your options. If you know you need as much money as possible and you were admitted to an institution that gave you a small scholarship, then that school is likely not the best fit for you.

The best way to pay for college is by applying for scholarships and grants. These are great because you do not have to pay that money back. There are a variety of scholarships available. Everyone from your local church to your college offers a chance for you to earn some tuition money. Everything from sports scholarships to academic and need based scholarships are awarded. Academic scholarships are the biggest group of scholarships given and are usually given by the school. There are companies and other groups that offer academic scholarships as well. If you receive a scholarship, these are some important questions you need to ask.

Is my scholarship renewable?

Some scholarships, especially ones given by the institution you are attending, are usually given over four years. However, some may be awarded for fewer than four years. It is important to know the terms of your scholarship so that you can plan accordingly. You don't want be in a position where you run into financial trouble because you did not know that one of your scholarships was non-renewable or not awarded for the entire four years.

Is the scholarship need-based or merit-based?

Need-based scholarships are exactly what they sound like. These scholarships are awarded based on the prospective student's need. These scholarships give students who may not be able to afford the full cost of tuition the opportunity to attend college. Research the requirements for need-based scholarships of the colleges you apply to determine whether you qualify for them. Even if you feel like you will not get anything, still apply for the scholarship. You never know what the result may be. The important thing to keep in mind about need-based scholarships is that if they are based on need, your need can change year to year, which may alter your scholarship. Colleges often determine whether you'll continue to receive these scholarships by reviewing the information provided on your FAFSA, which is based on you and your parent's income. So, if you get a job and earn money, or your parents get a raise at work, that may change your "need."

Merit based scholarships are given based on your accomplishments, such as high GPA, outstanding community service, letters of recommendations, and excellent testing scores. Sometimes you will have to write an essay on a certain topic, along with the other requirements, in order to receive this scholarship. The better your application and essay, the better chance of you receiving a scholarship.

My freshman year in college, I was able to pull through a 3.6 cumulative GPA. The following semester, due to the stress of taking 17 hours (with tough classes like organic chemistry, calculus, and biodiversity), my dad losing his job, and other personal issues, I finished my semester with a 2.75 GPA. Because my GPA was so high from freshman year, I was saved from losing my scholarship.

Is there a GPA requirement?

For renewable, merit-based scholarships, you might be required to maintain a certain GPA to keep your scholarship. The GPA requirement can vary at the university's discretion. It is up to you to find out that information so that you know what is expected when you start college. It is also important to know whether the GPA requirement is per semester or cumulative (an average GPA of all the semesters you have taken up to that point).

It's very important for you to maintain all scholarships that you are offered. Do not, we repeat, DO NOT believe that as long as you have the borderline GPA you will be safe. AIM HIGH! It may save you in the long run.

If I fail to meet one of the requirements for my scholarship is there a probation policy?

Some scholarships that have a GPA requirement may also have a probation policy. For example, a school may offer you a scholarship that requires that you maintain at least a 3.3 cumulative GPA. If you end the semester with a 3.2 cumulative, you will be put on probation and given time to raise your GPA. Check to see if there is a probation policy for your scholarship. If not, and you fail to meet the requirements, you might lose your scholarship immediately.

Other requirements (Ex. Community service hours, major, residency, etc.)

Other small requirements of merit-based scholarships may be given based on things such as community service, your major, your race and/or gender, or if you plan on working in underserved areas, etc. Knowing this information on the front end will help you know what is required to maintain your scholarship.

Stop, Breathe, Enjoy

So, you have gotten into college (yay!) and you are working through your decision-making process. What's next? Well, it is important that you pause and remember that you are rounding out your senior year of high school! This is your "last" year to make grade school memories with the friends that you have grown up with. Senior year brings prom, senior night (for our athletes & musicians), senior week, pranks and of course graduation! These events are designed to be fun and celebratory. During this happy time, it's important to maintain balance. In that regard, you must remember to enjoy these celebratory moments while maintaining your character.

STEP FIVE: Choosing the Particulars

We have FINALLY, arrived at step five! By now, we hope that you have selected a college and paid your seat deposit. Now, it is time for you to choose the particulars. Remember, you cannot choose the particulars until you have paid a seat deposit. Paying your seat deposit ensures that you are officially committed to a university.

Housing

One of the best things about college is that you get to live on your own. You no longer have to abide by your parents' "house rules," and you can start to make some rules for yourself. It is always good to have boundaries and set rules for yourself and others who live with you because it makes the living arrangement more enjoyable. As a freshman, you'll more than likely live in a dorm room that has about four people living in it. However, there may be some living spaces that only have two persons to a room or a suite. The best way to figure out where you want to live on campus is to figure out how you want to live, and whether you can afford what you want. If you want to live with a few people, then choose a living space that best fits that description. Be sure to also take into account other arrangements, such as community bathrooms, laundry areas, and how many people will be in that building. More people means more noise and higher foot traffic than you may be used to.

Roommates

It's almost guaranteed that you will be living with or in very close proximity to other people. If you are going to a school where you will not know anyone, you might be paired with someone you do not know. Although this could be scary, view it as a learning experience. You never know, the person who is your first roommate may become your best friend. If you and a friend are going to the same school, you can either choose to room with them or with someone else. Whether your roommate is a new or longtime friend, it's best to establish some things before you both move in. As soon as you find out who your roommate is, contact her to get an understanding of her preferences. See our resources section for a list of questions you and your roommate should work through.

Choosing a major

Talk to students who have your major that are upperclassmen to get help on what classes may be best to take your first year.

One important aspect of your college career is choosing a major. Some find this scary, but it can be fun and enlightening. First, look at programs that fit your interests or that will advance your skill sets for your career of interest. If you don't know what career field you want to pursue, then you can choose to be an "undecided" major. And that's okay! As an undecided major, you will have the opportunity to take general education classes (which all college students are required to take) until you are able to figure out which major is best for you. At most schools, first year students can only take general education courses their first year anyway. For those who do know what you are interested in, do not be afraid to claim that as your major early on. If you happen to choose a major your freshman year because you liked the subject area in high school and later realize you don't like it as much, you can change your major. Changing majors, however, sometimes means adding more classes to your schedule, which could cause you to spend an extra year or two in college. Although college is not a race, time and money is important. We advise that you try not to drag out your journey. So, be purposeful when it comes to choosing your major. Most degrees are achievable in two to four years depending on which college you decide to attend. Other degree options like Computer Science, Engineering, or any type of Advanced Science may automatically add another year or two to your college career because of the degree requirements. Do not shy away from choosing one of those majors if you know it is a good fit for you. Just be aware of major-specific requirements ahead of time.

Choosing Classes

Most of the classes you will take your freshman year will be general education courses (or "gen eds"). Starting off, there may not seem to be much variety in the courses you take. Keep in mind that it is best to start with the classes that are required. Closely monitor your paradigm or list of classes based on your program of study to figure out which ones are being offered or not. While you may meet with your advisor to discuss this, do not rely on your advisor to make your schedule. You must be proactive in making sure that you are taking the correct classes. Getting off track can result in a delay in graduating. Losing focus will likely lead to a schedule crowded with unnecessary classes and the possible loss of a scholarship.

You will have the freedom to take courses that are not strictly tied to your major; these courses are called electives. Electives grant you the freedom to take any class you'd like to take. Take some classes that you are interested in and take some that could help you advance in either your major or minor. Take classes that are fun, intriguing and even ones that challenge you to think more. Take classes that make you a well-rounded student. If you are an Engineering major, look for interesting History, English or Art classes. Why? Taking classes outside of your program of study will help you develop skills that you wouldn't normally use. Taking classes outside of your program of study can also help lighten the load from your required classes that might be more challenging as you advance. If you are a math major, most of your classes will be math classes. That type of repetition can be boring and a little daunting with all of the tedious details involved. Taking an art class, for instance, can help relieve some of the stress, by focusing your attention on something less demanding that has a different, more creative skill.

Stop, Breathe, Enjoy AGAIN!

We know this process can be overwhelming, but we have one more piece of advice before we move on to our next section. As you complete your final year of high school, remember that your character is your most valuable asset. Your character can cause doors to open or close. There have been many high school seniors that have had doors shut in their face because they participated in activities either during or outside of those celebratory events that destroyed their character.
Dear Brown Girl, don't let it be you! Keep your purpose and your future on the forefront of your mind. Remember that you have a bright future ahead and that

I spent time the summer before I went to college working for a dance company because this was a passion of mine. I love to dance and working for a dance company allowed me to travel and meet new people across the country. Additionally, because I applied to college "early acceptance", I received my acceptance letter right before Christmas, so the entire second half of my senior year I just was enjoying the end of year festivities such as Prom, senior week, and spring break! -Asia

the decisions you make right now can impact your future in ways unimaginable. The moral of the story is: just enjoy this season of your life, but remain purposeful in the activities that you choose to be engaged in.

Part One Pro Tips

Application Process

- FAFSA Applications open in October. Complete your FAFSA in October of your senior year of high school.
- Completing your college visits during summer allows you to visit colleges when your schedule is a bit more flexible. On the other hand, visiting colleges while you are in school will allow for you to see the university while courses are in session. Though this may cause you to miss class, most schools will allow for those absences to be excused. Make sure to check with your guidance counselor for your school's policy on attendance and college visits!
- The Common App opens August 1 each year. Gather all your application materials and be prepared to apply as soon as applications open.
- As you can see applying for scholarships is a continuous activity. Scholarship deadlines approach each month of the year. You should always be searching and applying for scholarships throughout the year.
- You can start researching schools as early as your freshman year of high school! If you start researching early you will need to update all factual information in your spreadsheet the summer before your senior year as this information changes each year. Researching schools early will help you in the long run!
- Compiling your list this way helps you save time during this phase of the application process. You will soon learn that this task will take a lot of time. Plan to work on your spreadsheet a little bit each day.
- Your goal should be to receive an acceptance letter AND scholarships.
- Begin preparing for your admission test the summer before your sophomore

year. Then take your test by the end of your sophomore year.

- You can also get your test answers and test questions back from the ACT. They will provide you with information on how they scored your test and all of the correct answers. It's called Test Information Release. For the SAT it is called the Answer Verification Services. This can help you figure out why you pick certain answers and what sections you need to improve on.
- DO NOT ask family members for letters of recommendation! This is frowned upon! Coaches, Volunteer Coordinators, Sponsors of Organizations you are involved in, are a great recommenders. Also, a teacher you received an excellent grade in or a class that you worked very hard to achieve the grade you received, and the teacher recognizes this are great examples of people you should ask for letters of recommendation.
- If your school does not offer test prep sessions, some churches and nonprofits have ACT/SAT Prep classes for free!
- Set calendar reminders on your cell phone to help remind you of any upcoming deadlines.

Making the Decision

Choose a school based on what YOU value! Make a list of what you like and dislike before making your visit! Self-Awareness during this stage of the application process is critical.

Part Two: When You Get There

Yay! You've made it to college!!! Time to celebrate, but also remain focused on the goal... GRADUATING & SECURING GAINFUL EMPLOYMENT. Remember that although college is a time to grow, make new friends, and explore who you are, it is also a time to find your purpose and begin fulfilling your purpose. In college, you will face familiar and unfamiliar challenges. This next chapter is dedicated to informing you of common things that you will encounter while in college. We have divided this chapter into sections based on topics and issues that students often face. The final section includes a discussion about on-campus resources that are generally included in your cost of tuition. Often, students fail to take advantage of these resources. We want to make you aware of what is available to you so that you can take advantage of the resources from the beginning.

The Academic

We started with academics because your primary reason for being in college is to further your education. No matter what you face, your academics should remain at the forefront of your mind. There will be things that will try to distract you from your studies, but you must remain self-aware and notice those deterrents as soon as they manifest.

From Mrs., Ms., Mr., to Professor

The learning environment in college is much different than the learning environment in high school. In college, you will be given a syllabus the first day of class and will be expected to keep up with your assignments and readings on your own. There will be less hand holding in college and you will be responsible for meeting with your professor to get help when you encounter difficult concepts.

On occasion, you will run into a difficult professor. Everyone has at least one difficult professor in their collegiate career. Below are a few strategies to deal with those professors.

Realize that this is reality. You will be dealing with challenges big and small as you go through life. This professor is not and *will* not be the only difficult person you will come across in your life. See this as an opportunity to grow and mature.

Do **NOT** let this person ruin your college experience. It may seem like the end of the world when you are dealing with it, but we promise it is not. Do not let one professor or one class make or break your experience.

Know who you are dealing with. Do some research on the professor. Figure out where their interests lie and make note of things they say or do in class that indicate their preferences. For example, if your professor indicates on her syllabus that she wants a certain type of citation or that she values classroom participation, then you need to conform your habits to their preferences. Likewise, If your professor loves talking about their research, then ask them about it. The more that you are on their "good side," the smoother your semester will be. Now, there is a fine line between creating good interactions and going overboard trying to flatter a professor. Be careful not to overdo things. **NEVER** become someone you are not, while trying to impress another person.

Remain professional. Keep your negative thoughts to yourself. It is ok to vent to a trusted individual about the professor, but do not go around telling the entire campus. Engaging in this type of behavior can ultimately taint your reputation.

Document everything. If a conflict arises it is best to communicate with the professor in writing. This protects you in the long run from any "he said, she said" disputes. Documenting a professor's conduct, or communications is key to effective conflict resolution.

Advising

As a student you will be assigned an advisor. Your advisor is the professor designated with the task of helping guide you through your academic journey. They are responsible for helping you choose classes, making sure you are on track to graduate, helping you find your career path, and making sure you have everything you need to graduate. Unfortunately, not all advisors are the same. If you feel like you and your advisor do not click, or if they do not have your best interest at heart, you can request to change advisors. Before you do that though, make sure that you are truly sure that your advisor is not for you, and make sure that your new desired advisor agrees to take on a new advisee. Ultimately, the burden of making sure that you are making satisfactory progress through your curriculum is on YOU. Often, students of color shift that burden to their advisor. It is their job to aid you through the process, but you must check to make sure you are meeting all of the requirements.

Grades

We know that grades are important because they have followed us, labeled us, and qualified or disqualified us since we started grade school. Do they still hold importance in college? As a matter of fact, they do. Grades determine your GPA, which can affect your ability to get into honor societies, summer programs, graduate schools, internships and sororities. It also plays a role in your financial aid which was discussed in part one. Make sure to visit our resources section to learn how to calculate your GPA.

Assessments: Midterms, Exams and Papers

In college, you will be assessed largely through midterms, exams and papers. Midterms happen in the middle of the semester. During this week, most of your professors will provide a test or paper that will cover what you have learned up until that point in the semester. Exams are similar to midterms except they typically have a higher weight on your final grade. They can also be cumulative, covering everything that you have learned over the course of the semester. Finally, papers are another form of assessment used by professors. Professors typically provide information on the topic of your paper and a rubric to explain how your paper will be evaluated. While midterms, exams and papers are common forms of assessment, please keep in mind that there are other forms of assessments that exist. No matter what type of assessment you are given, you should prepare well in advance, study hard and aim to perform your best.

In the spring of my junior year, I took Physics II. I soon learned that my professors teaching style was not my learning style. Going to my professor's office hours almost every day proved to be influential in my success in the course. -Paige

---

If you feel like your professor has a ton of students during office hours, email them and make an appointment! That way you can get more one on one time!

Office Hours

Office hours are times set aside by your professors for students to come get one-on-one assistance. Some students love office hours because they can get extra help and even pick the teacher's brain about topics for test questions. Others do not want or need to go beyond taking notes in class to learn and understand the topics. Students generally do not take advantage of office hours as much as they should. Using office hours for their intended purpose will give you an advantage in your coursework. Plan to spend time in office hours with all of your professors at least twice per month.

Learning Styles

The key to studying is knowing what your learning style is. Below is a lengthy discussion on learning styles. Read through the discussion and determine which learning style works best for you.

> *If your campus has a tutoring center, USE IT! Often times the tutors know the teaching and testing style of the professors and will be able to help you focus your studying. Take it from this former tutor!*

Visual

A visual learner picks up information best by seeing it. If you are a visual learner, things like graphs, pictures, and charts help more than reading a textbook. Doing hands on activities are also better for visual learners. Visual learners like using different colored pens and highlighters to help them remember the content. If you are a visual learner, studying somewhere with a white board so you can draw things out may be a good idea for you. Also, searching and watching videos on topics relevant to what you are studying should be helpful.

Auditory

An auditory learner picks up information by listening. They may not be able to understand by reading a book but listening to someone talk about the topic helps them understand better. If this is your learning style, going to lectures and taking notes may be less effective than recording lectures and re-listening to them. Most professors require consent before you begin recording. Make sure to ask your professor if you can record class lectures before actually recording them. If they refuse, try getting a tutor or visit the professor often during office hours so that you can hear the information repeatedly and ask questions.

Hands On/Kinesthetic

Kinesthetic or hands on learners are people who learn by doing. They can listen to you talk all day, but it is not until they are doing it themselves that they are able to master the concept. Kinesthetic learners struggle with this in college since most methods of teaching are lectures, not experiential. As a kinesthetic learner, you might try taking practice tests or quizzes to help you get that hands-on approach.

If after reading through the discussion on learning styles, you realize that your learning style might encompass a blend of the styles listed, that is okay! The best way to nail down your learning style is to experiment and see what works best for you. Also, consider that you may utilize one learning style in one subject area that may not be applicable to another class.

Studying

Now that we've gotten past that, let's talk about the particulars of studying. For the next couple of paragraphs, we are going to do a deep dive into studying. Resist the urge to skip this section. Studying in college will differ from studying in high school. The sooner you embrace that and put good study habits into practice, the more successful you will become academically. Before we dive in let's have a brief discussion about the class structure of college. In college, you will receive a syllabus. A syllabus outlines all the things the instructor plans to cover as well as the class expectations. Read it thoroughly. If the syllabus says read from a textbook, make sure you have access to the book, and you read prior to class.

Length of Time

Let's start with how much you *should* study. On average, you should be studying for one course at least twice the amount of credit hours your class is worth. So, if your class is 3 credit hours, you need to spend **AT LEAST** 6 hours a week studying for that class. Depending on how well you're doing in that class, you may need to devote more or less time to that course. Start with the recommended study time until you get a clear indication of how you are performing in the class.

Location

Where should you study? It's up to you! If you are the type of person that gets distracted easily, it may be best to get in a quiet space in the library. Some might feel more comfortable studying in their room. If you like to study in your room be careful of the obvious nearby distractions like food, the television and your nice comfy bed! Your study location depends on where you focus the best.

Studying in Groups or Alone

Studying is essential to doing well in college. Group studying can be beneficial. In groups, you have the opportunity to explain topics to each other and ask questions on material that you do not understand. Be careful with group studying. If you are not cautious, group studying has the potential to do more harm than good. On the other hand, studying alone is also good because it has less distractions and can help you understand the material in a way that will help you remember for the test. Below is a list of tips to help you have successful studying habits.

Keep your group small. After 3-4 people join the group, the study group is no longer a study group. It becomes a social gathering and it can be less helpful. Keeping your group at four people or less makes it easier to focus on the task at hand.

Studying with friends is not always the best option. We love our friends, but sometimes, studying with them can turn into a gossip session. If you decide to study with friends, make sure that they are as focused as you.

Have a plan. Group sessions are more successful when you have an agenda to keep you on task. One best practice is to break up the topics into different parts and hold each group member responsible for teaching that part to the rest of the group. Not only will that person be better at their topic, but it allows the rest of the group to ask questions and clarify unclear subjects.

Study with people who are doing well. If you are struggling in a course, it might not be wise to study with people who are also struggling. Do not be afraid to ask someone that is doing well if you can study with them. You are the company that you keep. Surround yourself with people that are reaching for the same goals as you.

Study by yourself. It is ok to say no to a group session if you prefer to study alone that day. Just remember to study with minimal distractions and remain focused.

Preparing for Tests

You should have some experience with taking tests in high school. College is not that far off. The difference is that you learn more information at a faster rate. The information is also more complex. Below are a few strategies to help you prepare for tests.

Find out the testing format. This can help you fine tune your studying. If the test is in essay format as opposed to being multiple choice, you will need to change your method of studying.

Once you find out the test format, figure out what you will be tested on. You can get this information by first looking at the syllabus and then confirming the topics with your professor. Separate the topics that you will be tested on and plan out when you will study each topic.

Doing practice questions is key to knowing whether you have mastered the material. If you are unsure of where to get practice questions, ask your professors for suggestions or look at the end of each chapter.

The Social

When you first get to college, you will be swamped with information about on-campus organizations you can join. Often, first year students fall into the trap of signing up for too much. Before committing to anything, narrow down your participation to maybe one or two major organizations that interest you. Doing this will give you the chance to devote more of your time to the organizations that you really like. There are also several opportunities to be social during college. We suggest that you focus on being purposeful and intentional when it comes to deciding which few clubs and organizations you will participate in.

Clubs & Organizations

During orientation and the first weeks of school, your college will likely host a student organization fair to offer information about the organizations on campus. We recommend that you visit each table to gather information. This will help you see which organizations fit you. Consider joining organizations that will allow you to explore different types of events and experiences. Many organizations focus on community service, leadership, and education. Choose to join a club that interests you and challenges you to grow.

Greek Life

Greek life, we have seen it, heard about it, or watched it on television. Believe us when we tell you that there is far more to Greek life than what is depicted in mainstream media. Sit back and take notes as we give you a comprehensive overview of Greek life so that you may make an informed decision.

We recommend that you read books, blogs, talk to members and talk to advisors at the university.

The biggest piece of advice that we can give about Greek life is for you to stay true to yourself. Make an informed decision that aligns with your values. Be true to yourself at all times, be yourself at all times and never succumb to the feeling to conform.

Sororities

No matter what school you choose to go to, there will be many options to choose from when it comes to Greek life. Sororities provide a great avenue for you to bond with a group of women who have similar goals and interests in life. Sororities help foster sisterhood, friendships, accountability partners, and they can aid in your overall development. If you are interested in joining a sorority, it is best to look at the values and goals of each organization that exists, and then make an informed decision. Don't pick a sorority based off of colors, events or even peer pressure. Choose the one that best fits with your morals and who you are as a person. Joining a Greek organization is a lifetime commitment, and you should treat your decision as such. If you join a sorority, prepare to be a part of a variety of social events, community service activities and networking opportunities. But most importantly, GRADES COME FIRST!

As we move forward in our discussion, we thought it would be important to provide a high-level overview of sororities. Sororities fall under three umbrellas. You have the National Association of Latino Fraternal Organizations, The National Panhellenic Conference and The National Pan-Hellenic Council. The National Association of Latino Fraternal Organizations was founded in 1998 and it houses 16 Latino Greek Letter Organizations. The National Panhellenic Conference was founded in 1902, and it is the umbrella organization for 26 organizations. The National Panhellenic Conference was founded at a time when women of color were not allowed in to college let alone into NPC sororities. Last but not least, the National Pan-Hellenic Council is the umbrella organization for the "Divine Nine" which is nine Black Greek Letter Organizations.

Making the choice to join any Greek letter organization is a huge decision. Make sure you do thorough research before joining any organization.

Fraternities

Fraternities are generally for guys, but there are some academic or discipline related fraternities that are co-ed. These groups are tailored to specific majors and career fields such as: business, pre-law, history, etc. These organizations are helpful, will prepare you to remain well connected in your profession beyond college and keep you up to date on the latest innovations in your field. Usually, students who join these organizations form study groups and network because of this similar interest or field of study.

Just like with sororities, Fraternities also have umbrella organizations. For the most part the umbrella organizations are the same as they are with sororities but there is one major difference. Instead of having the National Panhellenic Conference there is the Interfraternity Council (IFC).

The Professional

Urbandictionary.com defines "Securing the Bag" as "An expression used to describe the act of taking/obtaining advantage of the situation and keeping something of value." So what does that really mean? You are currently enrolled in college. Since you have this opportunity, take advantage of the situation and leave with something valuable. Your school has a wealth of opportunities that you can take advantage of. When you graduate from undergrad, there is NO excuse for you to leave with only a degree in your hands. When you walk across the stage, you should be able to reflect on the experiences you have gained, the meaningful relationships you have built with your peers and professors, and how much you have grown. And the list goes on and on. If you have not realized it yet, college is the time to secure the bag. Run to your nearest mirror and say, "I can have it all. I WILL have it all!"

Maximize Your time

For example, most winter breaks I was completing my applications for summer programs and researching additional scholarships. During the summer, I was at a summer program or internship. One of my spring breaks, I chose to visit professional schools with my career advising office. All of these experiences kept me ahead when planning for my after-college life. -Asia

If you are a traditional college student that plans to complete your degree in four years, then you have a total of four fall breaks, four winter breaks, four spring breaks and three summers. That may not seem like a lot, but it actually is! Many students get caught up in the habit of thinking that every break is turn up time. Yes, a break means it is time to relax, but you also need some time to work. You can stay ahead of the game if you use just a fraction of your time on breaks to get some work done. Be strategic about how you spend your time on breaks.

Opportunities: What, When, Where, Why & How

Where you go to school should not limit the type of opportunities that are available. If you begin to research some of the opportunities that we discussed and realize that they are not available at your school, do not stop there. Your school may use different terminology than we use. If your school does not have a specific program, reach out to someone to see if you or someone else can pilot the program at your school. Second, do not confine yourself to opportunities that are offered solely through your university. There are outside organizations and universities that provide programs and opportunities to college students.

The What: What types of opportunities exist?

Paid vs Unpaid

Deciding on paid versus unpaid positions can be tricky depending on your financial situation. If you choose a paid job opportunity, you will receive payment either weekly, bi-weekly, monthly, or at the end of the term via stipend. On the other hand, if you choose an unpaid internship, you will not receive compensation. Obviously, it seems like you should always seek out opportunities that will offer you some form of compensation. However, do not be afraid to take an unpaid opportunity because your "payoff" could be valuable in other ways. Some incentives for accepting an unpaid position include getting course credit, gaining professional experience and networking. To offset the financial gap, try applying for grants to help cover your living expenses. Also, you could work your unpaid opportunity part-time while working a paying part-time job. In other words, do not cross an unpaid opportunity off of the list just because it is unpaid. We have had some of the best opportunities of our lives working unpaid internships/volunteer opportunities. The truth is, there are many organizations that are willing to work with you and provide you excellent letters of recommendation. Some are just unable to pay you. (Is money your only motivation? It shouldn't be, brown girl!) Finally, if you decide to take an unpaid opportunity, do not let the employer take advantage of you. Hold your employer to the terms of the agreed upon hours and responsibilities, and make sure you document it all.

When I was volunteering at the hospital, I wanted to get an actual job so I could make money. My mother and mentor advised me to stay and take advantage. By working there, I was able to obtain a recommendation letter, meet other doctors, and was even on the news for my hard work! -Paige

Internships

What are internships? Internships are basically "mini jobs" that allow you to work for a fixed period of time in order to gain experience in a particular field. Some internships last for one semester, a summer or a year. Generally, the fixed period of time is up to the employer. Why seek out an internship? Internships are so valuable because they allow you to get real world experience in various fields. One thing you will come to learn as you take these next few steps in your life is that going to college is only one side of the coin. College coupled with real life experience is what all employers desire. Companies often spend little time "training" you on what you will be doing at work. You will be expected to adapt to the culture of the particular job. Working an internship will provide you the opportunity to get some real experience and become familiar with the work environment. Also, working internships gives you the opportunity to refine your interests. You will most likely be given a variety of tasks as an intern. As you work, you will have the opportunity to learn what you really like and dislike about different aspects of the job. This is valuable in the long-run because once you find something you like, you can take the time necessary to focus on your areas of interests.

Externships

Externships are similar to internships, but they tend to be more tailored to a student. Externships are for a fixed period of time. You may be able to receive course credit for participating in the externship depending on the university you attend. As a general rule of thumb, externships are unpaid. As far as the length of time goes, externships can last from one day to a year. It depends on your university and the employer. Externships are like opportunities to shadow an individual or employer. Externships are beneficial because they can count for course credit and give you the opportunity to learn from leading professionals.

Early Acceptance Programs

There are many colleges and universities that offer early acceptances into graduate or professional schools due to special affiliations. For example, my institution offered early acceptances to medical school in my sophomore year of college that students could take advantage of. There were of course some GPA and recommendation requirements, but it took a load off of people who knew exactly what they wanted to do after college. If you do take advantage of one of these programs, make sure you know all of the requirements and stipulations up front. Many require you to stay committed to their institution once joining the program. Therefore, if you are not sure that program is exactly what you want to do, you shouldn't apply. Additionally, there are many schools that offer preliminary acceptances into their graduate and professional schools before you even get to college contingent on specific test scores, so this is also something you may want to look into.

The When, Where, and How

The when, where, and how all fit together. When should you start looking for these opportunities? When do these opportunities actually happen? Where do these opportunities take place? Where do I go to look for opportunities? How do I apply for opportunities? How do I narrow my options? The answers to these questions can be found through research. Let's start with the how. How do you find these opportunities? There is a three-step process to finding out what is out there.

First, check your school email and check it often. Yes, yes we know. Half of the emails you receive from your school are probably worthless, BUT it is unlikely that your school will send you out an email with the subject line "LIFE CHANGING OPPORTUNITY PLEASE READ." Since the odds of that subject line coming to your email are not in your favor, then it is in your best interest to read each and every email. Sometimes finding the best opportunities are like searching for needles in a haystack.

Next, schedule some time with your career services office. Your campuses' career services office should be a central location for a variety of opportunities. Your tuition is funding the salaries of those who work in career services, so why not use what you already have to pay for? We recommend that you schedule a meeting with one of the professionals in the office. Tell them what your dreams and goals are and let them take it from there.

The last option is to start a search with good ole' Google. Chances are if you are reading this then you know how to use Google! We recommend that you spend some time in research, all starting with a Google search. If you are interested in going to law school, try searching "summer pre-law programs" and peruse through the results. Researching on Google can be time consuming, but it is 100% worth it.

After going through these three steps, the "how" leads you to the "when" and "where". By researching, you find out what opportunities exist, when they occur, and where they are located. Doesn't that all fit so nicely together? Now, when should you start looking for these opportunities? The answer is all day, every day. Because there are so many groups putting on activities, there will always be something going on. So do not miss out!

Networking: You have not because you ask not

"You have not because you ask not". As brown girls, we sometimes get so caught up in trying to not inconvenience people that we end up inconveniencing ourselves. We deserve opportunities just as much as the next person. Do not be afraid to ask for what you need or want. Email those professors for a good recommendation. Ask about that research project. Apply for that scholarship even though you don't think you qualify. Take advantage of every opportunity you have. You never know what you may get out of it!

Career Fairs

All students can take advantage of career fairs. You never know who you will meet that can help you find your intended career. When you go to these career fairs, it is important that you are dressed in business professional attire. This means a full suit, conservative heel (less than 3 inches), knee length skirt or slacks and an appropriate blouse. Bring copies of your resume and make business cards if possible. Sometimes, your career office can make the cards. If not, there are online templates that you can use to make your own. This will make you stand out when you meet different company representatives.

Business Attire: Blue, Black or Grey Suits (preferred)

If you cannot buy a full suit at the beginning of college, invest in a blazer with pants or skirts that match in color. Do not wear a top that has a plunging neckline or is too tight. Also stay away from tight skirts and pants. If you have to keep pulling your skirt down, then it's too tight. Keep jewelry simple. A pair of studs or small hoops and a necklace will suffice. Stay away from strong perfumes and body sprays. You want them to remember your qualities, not how much Bath and Body Works perfume you wore.

When the career fair is over, be sure to reconnect and follow up with the school or business representative via email. This will let them know that you are serious about being a part of their team, and they will remember you better.

> *My first suit came from the thrift store. You can grow your professional wardrobe by either shopping at the thrift store or gradually investing in suits as you attend more professional events. Eventually, I invested in about three different suits just because I was going to so many professional events. -Asia*
>
> ---
>
> *While at these fairs, always keep a positive and professional attitude. The person you talk to on the elevator or in the lunch line may be the key to that program you want to get into!*

Graduate School Expos

Business attire and a positive attitude are important when visiting a grad school expo, too. You do not really have to have your resume on hand if you are going to learn more about graduate schools. However, come with questions about programs that you are interested in, the application process, and program requirements. Make a good impression! These people see hundreds of students each day, so be sure to stand out in your own way! Again, follow up with the school representative after the fair and continue connecting with them. This may give you an advantage once the application process starts.

Shadowing

Shadowing gives you the opportunity to follow a professional to see what a day at their job looks like. It is a great way to see if what they do is something you want to consider for a career. When you shadow someone, it is important to dress in business attire (unless stated otherwise) and to be on time. "To be on time is to be late. To be early is to be on time." Make sure to arrive at least 15 minutes prior to your start time so that you show your enthusiasm and professionalism. Don't be afraid to ask questions; they are excited about their job and sharing their passion with you! After shadowing, be sure to send a handwritten thank you note to the career professional who hosted you. They will appreciate it, and it may help you in the long run!

Finding a Good Mentor

We often find it hard to obtain a good mentor. Some of us are interested in fields that are dominated by other races or the opposite sex. So how do you get started? Well, first let's cover what a good mentor is. A good mentor is someone willing to

If you don't know where to start or who to call, start local. For example, if you are interested in becoming a doctor, call up your primary care physician or pediatrician to get started!

One of my mentors is actually a neonatologist who basically sparked my love for medicine. He was always kind and encouraging and gave me tips I needed when applying to medical school. Even your advisor at school can be a mentor. My pre-med advisor was particularly amazing and always, I mean always, pushed me to my limits and always challenged me to do better. -Paige

invest in you and advise you to help lead you to success. You should be able to feel comfortable talking to them about your career goals, fears, strengths, weaknesses, and everything in between. They will encourage you and NEVER belittle you or be condescending. However, they will use tough love to push you to your limits. They actively help you find resources that you'll need to be successful. Plus, they are easy to connect with and contact.

A good way to start finding a mentor is to see who is in the field that you want to be in. Pay attention to how you interact with these people on a daily basis. Once you find someone you feel you connect with, don't hesitate to ask them to be your mentor. We're sure that they will be as excited as you.

The Financial

Budgeting

Unless you have an endless bank account that never runs out of money, you need to know how to budget. Budgeting is important because it allows you to plan your spending wisely so that you won't end up in debt. Most students are not swimming in money, so every dollar earned needs to be handled appropriately. So how can you get started?

One thing we want to discuss with you before starting the budgeting process is identifying the difference between needs and wants. A need is something that you cannot make it to the next day without. These things include a place to stay, food to eat, hot water to shower in, etc. A want is something that you necessarily do not have to have in order to function, such as that new pair of shoes you saw at Michael Kors.

Now, these two categories can definitely overlap. For example, you may need food, but maybe you should not go to Ruth Chris for dinner. On the other hand, new shoes are usually a want, unless you just put a hole in your boots and winter is just around the corner. It is your responsibility to discern the two based on what financial abilities you have. And budgeting is a great way to start.

We want to give you the basics on how to budget. You should try to adjust and update your budget at least on a monthly basis. Try to do it on the same day each month to make things easier. You can write it all out or make things easier by making a spreadsheet or using a budgeting app such as mint. We have listed below the factors you need to consider when making your budget.

1. Figure out your income. Most college students receive refunds. Refunds are money that is left over from scholarships and/or loans that are given to you by the college. Some of you may decide to work or have parents who give you an

allowance. Figure out the total amount that you receive per month and put it at the top of your list.

2. Take 1-10% of that income and save it. We would rather you start with 10%, but if that is a bit of a stretch for you it is totally ok to use a lower percentage. Just make sure that you are put aside the same amount of money each month. Even a dollar saved will give you $12 at the end of the year. Don't take any penny for granted. You may also consider opening a savings account to hold yourself accountable and to build interest. More on that later.

3. Calculate any one-time expenses. You may not have to get your car serviced every month, but you still want to account for it if you are responsible for paying the bill. This can also include books and other study material you get at the beginning of the semester.

4. Figure out your monthly costs. Monthly costs include rent, car notes, water and electricity, cell phone bills, and so on. Be sure to also include any monthly subscriptions you may have such as gym memberships.

5. Calculate the difference. Once you have calculated how much money you have coming in and how much you have going out. Calculate the difference by subtracting your expenses from your income. If the total comes out negative or even zero, then you need to readjust your expenses to make the number positive. That might mean that you have to cancel your Netflix subscription, but we want you to be debt free, you can watch Grey's Anatomy another time. If you do end up with a positive number our best advice is it to save it. You never know when an emergency may come up. You can also save it for future trips such as vacations or to just study abroad. You have choices when you don't live paycheck to paycheck!

So now that you figured out how to spend your money, where do you keep it? You can't put it in a box and bury in a yard, and you can't carry it on you at all times. We suggest opening up a bank account. There are two types of accounts you can have, a checking account and a savings account. You may choose to receive a debit card-which is the new check book-with a checking account. Savings accounts are not usually meant to be touched, and some banks use fees if you withdraw money from it too often. However, if you leave your savings be, most banks have an interest that will add money to your account, and who doesn't like free money?

When you set up an account, may sure you are aware of everything you need to make one such as important documents, a deposit fee, etc. Be sure to use a bank that is both in the location where you go to school, and where you are from. That will keep things simple and your family can put money into your account if you need it. Be sure to NEVER share your account information with anyone that you do not trust and be careful about logging onto your online banking account while on public, or unsecured Wi-Fi. Hackers have become very creative.

Last, we want to talk to you about credit cards. Fortunately, there are laws that forbid credit card companies from sending you credit card offers until you are 21, which has dramatically saved many students from falling into debt. We rather you not have one in college, but if you must, we advise that you use the following tips:

1. Try to find a credit card with fixed interest. This is hard to do but using a card with fixed interest keeps the company from suddenly increasing your rate and making it hard for you to pay off bills. Start by looking at bank credit cards and then venturing out.

2. Set a low limit on yourself. If you cannot pay your limit every month, then you need to lower it. So, if that means your limit needs to be $500, then so be it. The worst thing you can do is accept a ridiculously high limit and then never be able to pay it off.

3. Always pay off your balance each month. You should not see a credit card as extra money for you to use, simply because it is not yours. Credit cards are useful when shopping online or traveling because they have better protections against someone stealing your information and going on a shopping spree. It should NOT be used for when you run out of money. So only spend what you can pay back. Not only will this keep interest from making you $10 pizza jump up to $15 that you have to pay, but this also helps increase your credit score, which can affect your ability to buy things like cars, houses, and furniture.

Being a successful brown scholar means that we must manage our finances well and we hope this snapshot of how to do that will help you cry tears of joy when you graduate, not sadness.

The Personal

Friends, Haters and the In-between

"If someone shows you who they are, believe them" -Maya Angelou

One of the best things about college is meeting new people and establishing new relationships. This can also be the worst thing about college. When you dreamed about college as a high schooler, you probably envisioned an environment filled with mature adults and less drama. While often times this will be the case, more often than not, there is some drama. You will soon realize (if you have not already) that everyone who was your friend when you arrived, might not be your friend when you leave. Or friends you made in the beginning of your journey may not be your friend throughout the entirety of your journey. And that's okay!

As the years go by, you start to grow with people who have the same interests and goals as you. You also grow apart from those who don't. It just comes with growth and maturity. Those who care about you the most will understand that you cannot make every party because of studying, meetings, and other important school related matters. However, you will encounter those who won't understand and may become jealous of your focus, discipline, and success. Don't allow those people to discourage you. Your hard work is worth it! Each school year will bring new struggles and problems, but face them with courage and strength. Keep those you know are rooting for you close to you. Keep a distance from those who are obviously your haters. Be aware, though, that haters can very well be people who are a part of your friend group. They usually disguise themselves as someone who is supportive but are really negative when it comes to your efforts to excel in life. Be aware and cautious of those people.

Some people will never understand your drive to do something meaningful with your life. Don't let anyone get in the way of you doing what is right for you. This is your time to be selfish. This is a time to travel, start new adventures, and create new dreams. Don't get stuck because of people. Keep moving until you reach your destiny. Be greater than you thought you could be! Those who will be with you for a lifetime will follow, and those who won't will disappear. Keep going anyway!

Working in College

So you need extra money while you are in school? Or are you paying part of tuition out of pocket? Working during college is not an easy task; however, it is possible to keep a work-life balance. One way is to look for on-campus jobs such as work-study, tutoring, teacher assistant, resident assistant, or research assistant positions. These jobs typically pay well and often subsidize some of your educational costs. Another option is to find local jobs or part-time internships in your desired career field. For example, if you are planning on going to medical school, you could work at a hospital as a medical scribe part-time or work in a local clinic. If you can find a job that works with your schedule, that's great, but remember that school always comes first, so don't drive yourself insane trying to do both.

Work-life Balance

As mentioned earlier, work life balance is achievable and critical. The best way to stay organized is to keep a weekly schedule. If you have a calendar on your phone, set reminders for important assignments and meetings. If you don't have a calendar on your phone, try using wall calendars and planners; they serve the same purpose.

While planning, make sure to take time for yourself. It is easy to get caught up in assignments. However, it is equally important to do things outside of school work. Find a way to relieve stress and

I love to dance. So during college, I was part of a dance group on my campus. This allowed me to express myself creatively outside of the confines of the classroom. Join a workout class, go get a manicure, or hang out with friends. -Paige

---

My school started finals immediately after thanksgiving break and being six hours away from home sometimes, I had to make the decision to stay at school and study. -Asia

enjoy yourself.

In college, I was a biology major, so it was convenient for me to have a tutoring job, as it was a perfect opportunity for me to review information that I would be tested on in future standardized tests, such as the MCAT (Medical College Admissions Test). -Paige

---

Companies like Google and Microsoft have online calendars that will send you email reminders or even let you export your schedule. You can also have your schedule on your phone, laptop, and tablet for easy access! List all of your exam dates for the semester and major application dates for scholarships or programs on the wall calendar. You will have a daily reminder and visual countdown to keep you focused on how much time you should devote to studying and preparing for upcoming tests and assignments.

Family

Most of the time our family means well. But they often do not understand what college life is all about. Maybe you're a first-generation college student; maybe your parents did not have your major, or maybe you are in an entirely different state with a new culture. Whatever the case may be, there will be a few bumps in the road with family, and we want to offer you some advice to help you navigate those difficult situations.

Knowing when to say no and stay at school

You will have to set boundaries for your education. This will be tough if you are close with your family, but school is an investment, therefore it is important that you are fully invested in it. Family issues will arise, and when they do, you will have to gauge the importance and deal with them accordingly. You might be put in a situation where your family will want you to rush home, or you may be expected to come home every weekend. Setting those boundaries early on will help you deal with familial expectations. Keep at the forefront of your mind that going to college is similar to a full-time job. You will need to devote a significant amount of your time to your academics to have stellar grades, and you should make sure that your family understands that. If you need to stay on campus during a break, stay. If you need to miss a family gathering because of a school commitment, miss it. Your family may be hurt or upset at the moment, but we promise that it they will get over it.

Communicating with Family

You know your family best. You know whether they expect a phone call every day, or once a month. We cannot stress the importance of communication enough. No matter how busy you are you should maintain regular communication with your family. A simple text letting them know how you are doing can go a long way. There are two major reasons why this is important. First, your family cares about you. If they do not hear from you, they will be worried. If they are worried about you, there is an endless number of things that can happen. They may pop up on campus, or maybe even call campus safety to do a wellness check. You know your folks and what they are capable of when they are worried, so do not put them in the situation to worry. Second, communication is important because most students will still rely on their parents for financial support. If your family does not hear from you, they might be inclined to withdraw financial support. To avoid all of this, just call your family.

Dealing with Family Expectations

Expectations. We all have them for ourselves, and our families have them for us too. In college, you will want to make your family proud, and they will expect you to make them proud. But sometimes your family's expectations may be unrealistic, or they may not align with what your purpose for your life. If that is the case, you have to remember that when you graduate your name will be on the diploma, not your mom's, or dad's. Thus, you must feel confident in the degree program that you are enrolled in. You must have a passion for what you are studying, and you will need to have a desire to work in the career field that aligns with your degree. If at any point you realize that one of those factors has changed, you have to do what is best for you. Remember at all times that you can only be who you were created to be. Your family can have whatever opinion they want, but the opinion that matters the most is yours. Never let anyone make you feel bad for doing what you are passionate about or for doing the best YOU can do.

Let's be real, dealing with family is tough. It is even more tough when you are a young adult who still depends on their parents financially. Things will not always be perfect with family, but your family will always be your family so do what you can to maintain the relationship. Your family will sometimes want you to be perfect. But you cannot be perfect. Life is a journey, and it's not about how you fall but rather how you get back up and persevere. Do not compare yourself to anyone else and do not allow your family to compare you to anyone else. Stay in your lane. Stay focused. Live in your purpose, on purpose!

Balancing Relationships and Dating

Dating in college is usually inevitable. Whether you date the same person you dated in high school, or you date someone new, you need to be able to balance your relationship with school. Remember that school should be your first priority, but it is perfectly fine to date. Relationships can be a way to release stress and can help forget about the problems of school. However, they can also be a distraction if you do not know how to manage them. The best way to manage a relationship is by communicating with your partner. If you both go to the same school, make sure that both of you are focusing on school and your relationship. Hold each other accountable for your personal goals, school requirements and other achievements you both may have. Dating someone at your school is convenient but can also allow people to be in your personal business. People will want to know how you both are doing, will be watching how you interact with others, and will potentially try to influence your relationship. On the other hand, dating someone at your school, who motivates and encourages you, can help you navigate through your stress and be there for your successes.

Long distance relationships can be beneficial, yet distracting as well. These types are beneficial because it allows you to completely figure out who you are without the pressures of having a partner being so close to you. It also limits the distractions of having a partner near you at all times. The distractions come when you choose to spend more time video chatting, drive to see them, or staying up all night talking to them. Balance is key to a long-distance relationship!

Also, be cautious when dating someone who is not in school or not moving towards a goal in life. In these situations, your partner may not be supportive of your goals or will want you to spend more time with them than you can. They may also not understand why you have to achieve certain things or participate in different activities. If this is the case, it is best to have a conversation with them about how important your goals are to you. If this does not help the relationship, it may be best to leave the relationship. Stay focused on the tasks at hand and continue to do the best that you can do.

Dealing with a break up can be hard, especially in college. Don't let this hinder you from moving forward. It is okay to cry, be emotional and feel upset. But talk with your support system to help you through it. Channel that energy into something positive, learn from those lessons and continue to do what makes you happy. You are loved, and a break up should not stop you from reaching your greatest potential.

The Freshman 15 is Real Girl:

So, we are sure you've heard of the freshman fifteen….yes, it is real girl. How so? If you're a resident on your college campus, your meal plan allows you to visit the cafeteria multiple times during the day. You will also have the freedom to stay up late at night and eat. If you're not an athlete, you may actually become less active in college, leading to weight gain.

There are many ways to stay active during college and avoid the dreaded weight gain. The hardest part about staying healthy in college is maintaining a healthy diet. It is so easy to fall into the habit of eating late at night or ordering takeout from delivery food companies, especially when midterms and final exams come around. Try your best to resist the temptation by having a healthy diet and getting the proper amount of rest. Keeping your diet in line helps with your academic performance. However, if you do end up gaining the freshman fifteen (or the sophomore seventeen) you can always come back from that. The main goal is to feel good on the inside and to be comfortable in your skin no matter what size or weight you are. Make sure that you are just loving the skin you're in, girlfriend!

Take advantage of this because once you leave college, you realize how expensive gym memberships and personal trainers are.

Find a workout partner so that you guys can hold each other accountable as well as push each other to do better! Try healthy study snacks such as hummus and veggies or apple slices instead of chips and cookies.

Personally, I found I was stress eating. When I relieved my stress through exercise instead of Chipotle, I was instantly back down to my normal size. -Asia

---

I deal with general anxiety. I got to a point where I couldn't focus because I was too worried about the upcoming test. After I failed because I couldn't study, the cycle would just repeat itself.

Mental Health and Burnout

The mental health of women and people of color has recently been at the forefront of societal issues. Women of color are more likely to develop mental illnesses like anxiety and depression. We are also more likely to avoid seeking treatment due to stigma and other obligations. Brown girl, take you mental health seriously. Although college is fun, it is also easy to feel burnout from your courses. Recognize when you need help and ask for it. If you feel overwhelmed, have trouble staying focused, struggle with test anxiety, or just feel like you're losing passion for what you love, talk to a counselor or mental health professional. It does not mean you are crazy, it means you are human. Before starting classes, find out what resources your school offers to help you deal with stress and burnout. It may be hard to do at first, but it will help you reach your full potential that we know you have.

How to Deal with being Homesick

Feeling homesick is completely normal. It is important to find your home away from home. Find mentors, professors, and friends that are going to support you. Join an organization that brings people together from your hometown. While your friends may not come out and say it, trust us, they are missing home too. If you are struggling with being homesick, try scheduling weekly video-chatting sessions with family. Additionally, counseling services are usually available at every institution. Talking through your transition into college, homesickness, and concerns can really help.

I attended an out of state school. At first, the transition didn't seem hard; it got harder the longer I was away from home. So once I became a Junior and Senior in college, I really missed my family and home. Finding a home away from home was the key to me surviving homesickness. -Paige

On Campus Resources

When you pay for your tuition, you are also funding your access to on-campus resources. Many students fail to take advantage of these resources because students don't always know exactly what or how much is being offered to them. Make good use of these services. Just to give you an idea of what your campus may offer, below is a discussion about resources that are typically on every college campus. If you see something in the discussion below that you think might not be on your campus, reach out to your Dean of Students to verify.

Career Services

Every college is different about how they send out career opportunities. Nonetheless, most colleges and universities have a career planning office. Do not wait until you are a Junior or Senior in college to go to this office. Remember, your goal is to graduate and secure gainful employment. We suggest that you make an appointment with your Career Services Office within the first few weeks of school. Bring a copy of your resume to this appointment and allow the staff members to review your resume and give you feedback. In this session, you should also make the staff aware of your long-term goals and inquire about internship, externship and shadowing opportunities. Your career services office knows about unique opportunities just for students. Career Services exists to help students secure employment both during school and after graduation. Let them help you!

Student Life

The name of your Student Life Office will vary depending on the institution, but this office is the hub for residency, student organizations and the student experience. What is great about this office is that they also provide student excursion opportunities to other cities, museums, and cultural events. If you have any questions about student organizations or student involvement, this is your go-to office.

Health Services

Your university likely offers health services as well. Most campuses will have a nurse on staff that you can visit if you become ill. Larger universities may have doctors on staff as well. Whether large or small, you should take advantage of these health services before running off campus to see a doctor. These services are generally free for students and are easily accessible. Also, universities typically have counselors on staff to help students. Your mental health is so important! Do not feel like you can only take advantage of this resource if something is going wrong in your life. Use these services year-round!

Disability Services

Finally, we could not end this section without discussing disability services. Typically, when people think about disabilities they think about physical disabilities. We want to challenge that perception. There are a plethora of invisible disabilities what people around the world struggle with. No matter what campus you choose to attend there will be disability services. If you have been diagnosed with a disability, then you need to make sure you get the appropriate accommodations for your academic services. At a minimum you should check in with this office once per year.

If during the course of your study, you feel like you are having issues, or you get diagnosed with a physical or learning disability or you have a change in your health you should check in with the disability office to see if any of their services would be of help to you.

Part Two Pro Tips

The Academic

- Realize that dealing with difficult people is the reality of life.
- Do not let difficult professors ruin your college experiences.
- Make it a point to know who you are dealing with. Research your professors, know their likes and dislikes.
- Never become someone you are not, while trying to impress another person.
- Remain professional. Keep your negative thoughts to yourself.
- Document everything. If a conflict arises it is best to communicate with the professor in writing.
- College is much different in high school. When contacting professors verbally and in writing make sure to use the appropriate title. In college "Ms. Mrs. and Mr" are no longer used. Instead use Professor, or Dr.
- Talk to students who have your major that are upperclassmen to get help on what classes may be best to take your first year.
- If you feel like your professor has a ton of students during office hours, email them and make an appointment! That way you can get more one on one time!
- If your campus has a tutoring center, USE IT! Often times the tutors know the teaching and testing style of the professors and will be able to help you focus your studying. Take it from this former tutor!
- If you like to study in your room be careful of the obvious nearby distractions like food, the television and your nice comfy bed!
- Keep study groups small, and always have a plan for what you will study.

- Studying with friends is not always the best option
- Once you find out the test format, figure out what you will be tested on. You can get this information by first looking at the syllabus and then confirming the topics with your professor.

The Social

- We recommend that you read books, blogs, talk to members and talk to advisors at the university.
- The biggest piece of advice that we can give about Greek life is for you to stay true to yourself. Make an informed decision that aligns with your values. Be true to yourself at all times, be yourself at all times and never succumb to the feeling to conform.

The Professional

- While at these fairs, always keep a positive and professional attitude. The person you talk to on the elevator or in the lunch line may be the key to that program you want to get into!
- If you don't know where to start or who to call, start local. For example, if you are interested in becoming a doctor, call up your primary care physician or pediatrician to get started!
- My first suit came from the thrift store. You can grow your professional wardrobe by either shopping at the thrift store or gradually investing in suits as you attend more professional events.

The Financial

- Set a budget and stick to it
- Find a credit card with fixed interest and maintain discipline by setting a low limit on yourself.
- Always pay your full monthly balance.

The Personal

- Some people will never understand your drive to do something meaningful with your life. Don't let anyone get in the way of you doing what is right for you. This is your time to be selfish. This is a time to travel, start new adventures, and create new dreams.
- Keep moving until you reach your destiny. Be greater than you thought you could be! Those who will be with you for a lifetime will follow, and those who won't will disappear. Keep going anyway!
- Keep a weekly schedule!
- Companies like Google and Microsoft have online calendars that will send you email reminders or even let you export your schedule. You can also have your schedule on your phone, laptop, and tablet for easy access! List all of your exam dates for the semester and major application dates for scholarships or programs on the wall calendar. You will have a daily reminder and visual countdown to keep you focused on how much time you should devote to studying and preparing for upcoming tests and assignments.
- Take advantage of this because once you leave college, you realize how expensive gym memberships and personal trainers are.
- Find a workout partner so that you guys can hold each other accountable as well as push each other to do better! Try healthy study snacks such as hummus and veggies or apple slices instead of chips and cookies.

Part Three: What's Next?

Can you picture being close to the finish line? Graduation season is a fun time! If you are like us, you'll be excited to be completing one phase of your life and anxiously excited for what's to come. For most of your life, the plan has been laid out for you. Finish high school, go to college, and then graduate. Once you've been through almost four years of college, you will realize that your interests may have broadened. There is a great big world out there with so many opportunities that you will want to grasp. Your opportunities after graduation are truly endless. We suggest that you begin thinking about those post-grad opportunities during the spring of your sophomore year. That way if you want to go to graduate school, you will have enough time to prepare for admissions tests. Or if you want to take a gap year, you can take a gap year by choice, not by force. Feeling a little confused about those post-grad plans or do not know where to start? Do not worry! You have many options, and we are here to share a few!

Option 1: The Gap Year

Some graduates leave college unsure of what they want to do, or they may just be in need of a little break before graduate/professional school. This break is what we call a gap year. There is nothing wrong with taking a gap year or two. However, we want to caution those who may be considering a gap year as an option. Your gap year should be filled with doing something productive. Do not think that a gap year is a time for you to just chill. If you choose to take a gap year, be productive and make the most of it. Awesome ideas for gap year opportunities include working a job in your desired career field, working for a non-profit, and applying for fellowships. You could also take time to travel. Taking time to travel is a good way to spend your gap year because once you start your career, it may be harder to travel. If you weren't able to travel abroad as an undergraduate, you can take this time to see the world, meet new people, and learn about new cultures. This will make you more well-rounded.

Option 2: Graduate School

Most STEM graduate school programs are funded through external grants and the university. For these programs, you should mainly only look for funded programs because most are funded.

The earlier you start, the less stress you'll have at the end!

After college, you may further your education by attending graduate or professional school. It's best to start thinking about grad school the first semester of your junior year. Starting at this point will allow you to be more prepared, get ahead with choosing the right school, knowing which tests to take, and determining which program is best for you. Once you decide that you want to attend graduate school, you need to choose a program, and come up with a list of schools. Look for schools that offer high rated, cost efficient programs that would further your undergraduate degree. Cost should be a factor when looking at grad schools because they can be expensive. When looking at your options, choose the option that works best for you. Grad school is more serious than undergrad. It will have higher standards for completing the course, including making higher grades to remain in school. Nowadays, an undergraduate degree, in many study realms, is not enough to be successful. Most companies are looking for master's degrees, PhDs and other certifications because it shows that one has more knowledge in their field and has gained specialized experience. So, it is great if you are considering attending graduate or professional school!

Most grad schools require specific tests such as: the GRE, MCAT, LSAT, etc. These tests can be extremely hard and expensive; thus, you will need to start preparing for them earlier than your senior year. Some of these tests are offered less frequently so you only have a few chances to take them. Also, some tests have limitations on the amount of times you can take them.

Planning and studying earlier will give you some wiggle room if you need to take the test multiple times, and it will lessen your load when it comes to senior year. Starting early also gives you enough time to acquire a great score to include in your application well before graduation.

Dual Programs

Some professional or graduate schools allow for people to get two degrees at once. The student's work for the university will be used for two degrees instead of one. Generally, this means completing both degrees in less time, but may add classes. For example, law schools allow students to get their Juris Doctorate (J.D.) and Master of Business Administration (M.B.A.) at the same time. Certain business law classes can be used towards the M.B.A., which means taking less law classes overall, but will add M.B.A. classes. Also, a traditional J.D. program is three years and a traditional M.B.A. is two years. With the dual degree program, it is traditionally four years. This is a great idea for those who want to finish more than one degree for the price of one depending on the school. The years may vary depending on the school's program or how quickly you want to finish. Some schools may even allow you to get another degree from a different school if they partner with the school for that particular program. If you are interested, it is best to ask the admissions counselor as you inquire about the school.

Accelerated Programs

An accelerated program allows you to finish your degree quicker. The time varies based on the school's requirements. For example, law schools are typically three years. However, participating in an accelerated program might mean two years. Accelerated programs sheds a minimum of a year off but can be rigorous and challenging. Talk with you admissions counselor and students in the program to see if this is an option for you. The pros are finishing quicker and starting work sooner, but the cons could mean year-round classes and a faster pace without much room to slow down.

Conditional Programs/Acceptances

Conditional programs are non-traditional avenues to enter grad school. These programs are set-up to give more people a chance to attend grad school. These are usually for students who have not met the standardized tests scores but have a strong academic and college presence. If your school asks you to participate in this program, do it! It does not mean that you are not smart enough, but it gives you insight on how the program will be. These typically take place in the summer before the fall semester starts. You will take classes that are a part of the program, will do homework/assignments and will have to take an exam to see if you will be successful in the program. If you prove that you can succeed, you will likely be admitted. If not, you will either be referred to completing the program again or will receive a rejection letter. However, these programs are created to get you in! Schools that have these programs leave a certain number of seats and as long as you do your best, you will likely get in. Think of this as a learning opportunity that students who were already admitted may not have. It will help you understand how the program runs, how the classes are taught and how you will be graded once you start in the fall. These programs give you an advantage, so take it if it is offered to you!

Option 3: Deferring grad school acceptance

Many graduate schools will allow you to defer your graduate school acceptance if you receive a prestigious fellowship or grant. A deferral is delay in admission after a person receives their acceptance; one might work, travel, or do something else for a year before matriculating. Keep in mind that it is at the school's discretion whether or not they will grant you a deferral for a year. You will need to communicate with the school to learn what their policies are for deferral.

Option 4: Fellowships

Fellowships are opportunities that allow students to do research and assume the position of a teacher or graduate assistant. A fellowship could also be a position that helps you gain more experience in your field of study. A fellowship allows you to make meaningful connections and work closely with professors, other researchers, various organizations, and other fellows. These positions are usually limited and given to unique individuals who are dedicated. Fellowships also require a certain GPA depending on the program requirements. Receiving a fellowship of any sort is an honor and should be taken seriously. If you are accepted, have fun and make this experience one of learning and growth. It'll set you apart from your peers and will help you to establish relationships with people who can be great assets to your future career.

Option 5: Post-Grad Internships

Post-graduate internships are like internships that you may have worked during undergrad. If you need a refresher on internships go back to part 2. The major difference between post-graduate internships and internships while in college is that post-graduate internships will likely be full-time, as opposed to part time.

Option 6: Working after Undergrad

Some companies only require a college degree and will most likely hire you after graduation depending on your major and skill set. Students choose to work after graduation to give themselves a break from school. Some careers don't require you to further your education beyond a 2- or 4-year college, so starting a career after graduation, for many, is inevitable. It's best to choose a job that you can see yourself growing and gaining valuable experiences in. If your first job is not in your field of study, do your best at it and still take it seriously. Use that job experience to gain and develop personal and technical skills that you don't already have. You will develop into a more well-rounded person. Bringing those skills to your career will help set you apart from your co-workers and prove that you are capable of working in various areas.

Option 7: Working & Grad School

Some jobs will pay for their employees to further their education while working. This is a great incentive because you get to work and go to school essentially for free. The job may ask you to work a certain number of months before being able to start school, but it's a good investment. If you don't have this option and must work during grad school to be able to pay for it, that's okay! While working, make sure you manage your time well and do your best in school and your job. If work is more demanding, take one or two classes to ensure that you can keep your grades up. If work is flexible and works with your school schedule, you may be able to take more classes. However, keep in mind that most grad schools require at least a C to pass the class.

Transitioning to Adulthood

If you thought you were grown when you turned 18, you were wrong. The real adulting begins once you graduate college. The free stuff comes to an end, your school starts pestering you about donations, and if you have loans…well more on that later. Honestly, adulting is something that NO ONE has perfected, except maybe Beyoncé (but she's freaking Beyoncé).

The best advice we have for anyone that is transitioning into adulthood is to stay organized, remember your purpose, and realize that you will make mistakes. If you haven't been doing so already, you will have to remember to pay bills, make your own appointments, schedule time with family and friends, find time to exercise, and still somehow go to work or graduate school.

You will have to balance a lot while adulting but remember to TAKE A BREAK. Sis, burnout is real. We are some of the hardest working and underestimated people on the planet, and that is a lot to deal with. Meditate, go to the gym, go get that facial, or just have lunch with your best friend. Do what you need to do to separate yourself from your work and responsibilities, even if just for an hour. It will make the difference. Just be careful not to overindulge and get off focus - there's still goals to accomplish!

Another thing we would like to point out that brown girls tend to struggle with is asking for help. We love to do everything on our own, either because we think no one else will get it done in a timely fashion, or even because we feel like we inconvenience others when we ask for assistance. The best thing to do when you know you need help is to ask for help! Remember, we have not because we ask not. How useful can you be to your community and workplace if you're burnt out from taking on too many responsibilities on your own? The answer: completely useless. So brown girl, ask others for help, and then, allow them to help you.

Paying on loans?

Whew chile! Loans... almost everyone needs them, and no one wants to have them. So for those of us who do need them, how exactly does paying them off work? Here are a few options.

Get ready to pay- About 6 months after you graduate, your first payment is due. How much you pay depends on how much you borrowed. It also depends on the interest rate that you have, which can change each year. If possible, try to pay on the interest BEFORE you actually are required to start paying on your loans. This will decrease the amount of interest you have to pay in the long run, which is what hurts most graduates.

Defer your payments- If you are planning to go to graduate school and plan to take out loans for that program as well, you can defer your payments until you graduate again. This means you don't have to worry about paying on your loans while furthering your education. . If you receive loans through the government, they usually try to keep all of your loans under the same company, which is helpful.

Sign up for a loan forgiveness program- If you are an aspiring teacher, doctor, or police officer, keep in mind that some schools and cities have programs that will pay off your loans if you serve the community for a certain number of years. Be sure to do your research before making the commitment. Some programs still require you to pay on your loans while you're working and will just pay off whatever is left after you are done with your service term. The same applies for military programs.

If at all possible, try to get your loans through the government. They have rules regarding interest rates and methods of paying back the money you owe. Private loans are different.

Starting a new career?

Starting a new career can be an intimidating experience. You may feel like you have to prove yourself to your boss, your coworkers, and even yourself. Brown girls are almost always underestimated, and we have to work twice as hard to get half as much. How can you continue to be successful without losing yourself in the process?

First, stay positive. Negative thoughts only produce negative actions. If you constantly complain about your job, you will come to hate it. Speak life and positivity into your career. Use each challenge as a way to prove your worth and strength. Don't give anyone a reason to doubt your abilities.

Second, take your job seriously. "To be on time is to be late. To be early is to be on time." You won't make a good impression if you are late to your job and meetings, even if it's by a few minutes. Plan to arrive at least 15 minutes early in order to give yourself time in case something comes up, such as a travel delay.

Also, be kind to everyone. You never know what role they will play in your future. Keep your friends close and your enemies closer. If it appears that someone is trying to make your experience a negative one, respond with positivity. They want you to react in a negative way; don't give them that gratification.

Lastly, have fun! You chose this career for a reason. Remember that reason when you feel overwhelmed by a plethora of deadlines. Remember that reason when your superior is giving you a hard time. Remember that reason when your least favorite coworker keeps stealing your chips out of your bottom right desk drawer. You've worked hard to get to that point. Enjoy the fruits of your labor.

Part Three Pro Tips

Part 3

- The earlier you start on your post graduate plan, the better!
- Take breaks, burn out is real!
- The best thing to do when you know you need help is to ask for help! Remember, we have not because we ask not. How useful can you be to your community and workplace if you're burnt out from taking on too many responsibilities on your own?
- Be prepared to pay off loans six months after you graduate.

A Final Word

Hey Brown Girl, as we bring this guide to a close, we want to offer a little bit of encouragement. You are in such an amazing season of your life. You are about to experience some of the best years of your life. We can say this with confidence because we have been through it. We made this guide because you deserve to know just as much about college as your classmates. You are so unique, and you are on this earth for a purpose. You may not know your purpose just yet, but if you just sit and think about it; you have experiences, knowledge, and connections that will ultimately help you get to where you need to be. Do not fall into the temptation to compare yourself to others because you were created to have a unique path. The ultimate goal is to continue pushing and striving for greater while enjoying the journey.

You may be a first-generation college student surrounded by classmates that are in the lineage of college and professional school graduates. After reading this guide, none of that matters because you've been prepared. We wanted to share our "secrets" with you. Acing college and unlocking opportunities for professional success should not be a secret kept from students of color. We genuinely want you to succeed and walk in your purpose, and if college is one of the steps necessary to make your dreams come true, then this guide is a necessary resource to give you the tools you need to get to where you want to go. There is enough room for all of us at the top, and we want to help you get there.

xoxo,

Taylor, Amber, Paige & Asia

Resources

Career Assessments

Princeton Review, https://www.princetonreview.com/quiz/career-quiz

Career Goals

College Board, https://bigfuture.collegeboard.org/explore-careers

Education Goals

College Board, https://bigfuture.collegeboard.org/find-colleges/college-101/quick-guide-your-college-degree-options

Fee Waivers

Qualifications for an SAT or ACT fee waiver:

-Enrolled or eligible for the National School Lunch Program

-Family income is within the USDA Food and Nutrition Service Income Eligibility

-Enrolled in any state, federal, or local program for students from low-income families (Examples: Upward Bound or TRIO)

-Your family receives public assistance

-You live in federal subsidized housing, a foster home, or are homeless

-You are a ward of the state or an orphan

Note: These fee waivers are only eligible for 11th and 12th grade students with an exception of the SAT subject tests which are open to 9th-12th graders

This information is something you will have to discuss with your school counselor in order to get approval. For more information:https://collegereadiness.collegeboard.org/sat/register/fees/fee-waivers

http://www.act.org/content/act/en/products-and-services/the-act/registration/fees.html

SAT Subject Tests

What are SAT Subject Tests?

These tests are required by very few schools. However, if a school that you are interested in requires them, then they may specify which ones you need to take or you can choose the ones you believe are your strongest subjects. I actually took two subject tests myself in the subjects I took AP classes in. I was most prepared for these subjects since I already had to take a comprehensive test over the material. The registration fee is $26 for up to three subject tests on one test day.

FAFSA- Free Application for Federal Student Aid

Fafsa.ed.gov

This is the only official website to apply for federal student aid. Please DO NOT go to any other website because they may scam you by trying to retrieve some of your vital personal information or making you pay money to do an application. The FAFSA is completely FREE

If you decide to accept loans for college, you need to know these three types:

Direct Subsidized Loans- For undergraduate students who have financial need. Can borrow up to $5,500. No interest is charged on the loan as long as you are at least a half-time student (6 credit hours per semester). Interest rate is 5.05%*

Direct Unsubsidized Loans- For undergraduate, graduate, and professional degree student with or without financial need. Can borrow up to $20,500. You are responsible for the interest even if you are full time. Interest rate is 5.04% for undergraduate and 6.6% for graduate/professional students.

Direct PLUS Loans- For parents paying for their undergraduate child's tuition or for graduate/professional students with or without financial need. Can borrow up to the cost of attendance at the institution (tuition, room and board, etc.). Interest rate is 7.6%

*Please note that the interest rate is subject to change on a year to year basis. However, whatever the interest rate is when you borrow is what you will pay, not

what the interest rate is once you *start* paying.

Document Writing

Example of Email to Professor, etc. asking for a Letter of Recommendation

Good Morning Dr. Jones

I hope this email finds you in good spirits. I am emailing you to ask if it would be possible for you to write a strong and positive recommendation letter for college. I will be applying to enter next fall, and I would be very grateful if you wrote a recommendation letter. Please let me know if this is feasible at your earliest convenience. I hope to submit my application by October 15.

Thank you for your consideration and I hope to hear from you soon.

Sincerely,

Jane A. Doe

Example of a Good Recommendation Letter

To whom it may concern:

This letter serves as a recommendation for Miss Janet Doe. I have had the distinct pleasure of knowing Janet for three years as a student and as a cheerleader on my Cheer Varsity Squad. Janet has been more than the ideal student and individual. In order to reach my level of standards and deepest respect, Janet has maintained commendable grades and values throughout the time period that I have known her.

The academics at Central High School are rather challenging, yet Janet has met that challenge by taking a host of honors and advanced placement classes while remaining a high GPA. Not only is she a scholar, but Janet's success ranges in the extracurricular department as well. She is the Captain of the Central Cheer Squad, a member of Central's illustrious National Honor Society, and a member of other various organizations.

Janet Doe not only represents her school, but her community as well. During the summer months, she serves as a volunteer dance instructor. With an interest in Biology, she also makes sure to work at the Women's Hospital gaining knowledge on her prospective career.

Since her classmates, my fellow teachers, and I will always hold her at the highest pedestal, I sincerely recommend Janet Doe as the ideal candidate for your scholarship.

Sincerely,

Cheer Coach

Example of Resume/Brag Sheet

Janet A. Doe

1234 W. 3rd St., Chicago, IL, 12345 * (123)-456-7890 * JanetDoe@gmail.com

Education

University of Illinois at Chicago (UIC) – Chicago, IL *August 2017-present*

Masters of Public Health, candidate – *Maternal and Child Health concentration*

Xavier University of Louisiana – New Orleans, LA *May 2017, BS Public Health*

Volunteer Experience

Tutor – Mobilization at Xavier (M.A.X.): Teaching Young Children (TYC), New Orleans, LA – *April – May 2016*

As a member of TYC I volunteered with elementary school children, primarily 2nd and 3rd graders, after school and aided their teacher in any activities that had been planned for that day. I would read them stories, do arts and crafts, or help them with homework assignments while they waited on their parents to pick them up.

Tutor – Mobilization at Xavier (M.A.X.): Homework Clinic (HWC), New Orleans, LA - *September – December 2016*

As a tutor in HWC I volunteer at Xavier's off campus community center tutoring children who attend neighboring elementary school with their homework. I tutor on Mondays, Tuesdays, and Wednesdays for two to three hours working with the children and aiding them in the math, reading, spelling, or science homework that they are assigned with.

Work experience

Independent Birth Doula – *Chicago,* IL – *December 2017 – present*

As a birth doula, I take on private clients (expecting mothers and their families)

and support them through their pregnancies with prenatal education visits, which consist of the discussion and planning around the stages of labor, coping mechanisms for comfort and pain, breastfeeding education, and how to prepare for postpartum life with a new baby; continual support throughout the labor period until the delivery of the baby, and initial postpartum support with adjusting to life as a mom, breastfeeding, and other comfort measures.

Dance Instructor – Out of School Club, Chicago, IL - *Summer 2014, 2015, 2016, 2018*

Out of School club is a *Safe Haven* for inner city children on the west side of the city of Chicago. I was the dance instructor for the program for three consecutive years, where I taught both the young girls and the young boys full length choreography that encompasses different dance styles and techniques such as: modern, ballet, hip-hop, contemporary/lyrical, and West African dance. At the end of the summer program the children put on a one-hour performance for their family, friends, and community exhibiting the crafts and skills they had learned during their time at camp.

Skills

Leadership

- Served as Public Health Student Association (PHSA) President, *Fall 2018 – Spring 2019*
- Entrepreneur as an independent birth doula, *December 2017 – present*
- Small group leader/facilitator at Soul City Church, *October 2017 – present*
- Served as Xavier Campus Ministry Liturgical Dance leader/co-leader, *Fall 2012 – Spring 2017*
- Served as Xavier Campus Ministry Bible study co-leader, *Spring 2013 – Spring 2017*

Honors/Awards

- Truman Capote Literary Award/Scholarship recipient – *Awarded Spring 2016*
- Dean's List, Xavier University – *Awarded Fall 2016*

- Lisa McClain Service Award – *Awarded Spring 2017*
- Center of Excellence in Maternal and Child Health Scholarship Awardee – *Awarded Fall 2017 & Fall 2018*

BRAG SHEET

List the clubs and organizations you were involved in from 9th grade:

Organization Name	Years involved	Leadership Position

List any Volunteer Activities:

Activity/Organization	Role	Dates

Hours

List any Work Experience:

Employer	Dates	Job

Description

Extracurricular Activities:

Activity	Dates	Hours

Awards/Honors:

Name of Award	Date	Description

Three words to describe positive qualities about yourself:

Future Goals:

Additional Information about yourself that would be helpful to the letter writer:

Personal Statement Samples

Prompt I: The lessons we take from obstacles we encounter can be fundamental to our success. Was there a time when you faced a challenge, setback, or failure? How did it affect you, and what did you learn from the experience?

Failure can be the best teacher. I know this because I failed, and I learned more from it than from any of my successful experiences. It all started with an F. Getting an F probably isn't the worst thing in the world, but it's not something anyone wants to see on their transcript. I received it a few days after taking the first history test of the year. This was the test my teacher confirmed was a third of my grade. I immediately thought my chances of being accepted into a four-year college was over, and I had just started the school year.

I didn't know what happened. I'm not an F student. I've only gotten one C. F's are out of character for me, and it got my attention. However, I knew I didn't study, but I thought I knew the material well. Once I sat down to take the test, I realized I wasn't as prepared to take the test as I thought. I had two options. I could accept that I was not as great of a student despite what I had thought. Or I could study extremely hard for the next test and bring my grade up. I realized something important: I had forgotten the reason why I didn't study but not the grade. Thus, the grade itself was far more important than how I felt at the moment and the reason for not studying.

If I had gotten a B or C rather than failed, I would have learned nothing. Or, at the very least, I would have learned that I didn't have to study, which is the opposite of what any college-bound senior should learn. I chose to work harder. By my failure, I had already learned the consequences of not studying. I knew both the problem and the solution. It didn't make it easy. I steadily brought my grade up with subsequent tests and papers.

At the end of the year, I got a better grade than I should have, based on statistic. The teacher weighted improvement over other concerns. Those who buckled down and worked harder as the year progressed were rewarded. In essence, my hard work paid off. Had I not failed, I would have learned nothing. I might have done much worse on a later test, if I "knew" studying was not important. Instead, by failing, I was able to learn from the experience. Going into college, I now know how important hard work can be.

Prompt II: What diversity do you plan to bring as a student at our university?

Thinking about diversity reminds me of a puzzle. Although the pieces are contrasting, those differences fit together to form a beautiful work of art. Despite the differences, they have something in common; they work together to reach the concurrent goal of making an image. In life, we are the pieces. We are all distinctly different, yet we share similarities. Anne Frank validated this when she said, "We all live with the object of being happy; our lives are all different yet the same. Happiness is different for each individual person; however, we all know that happiness is what we want to achieve."

Anne Frank's *Diary of a Young Girl* had a vague significance to me when I read it during middle school because I had not branched out of my community to experience new cultures. I was born and raised in Memphis, Tennessee, a place where the culture, climate and mentality of the locals is unique from any other city. Ironically, I was raised in a household where diversity was nourished and cultivated.

My parents constantly encouraged me to encounter experiences beyond Memphis. They always inspired me to be exposed to the unknown. It is different when you actually experience disparities in cultures first hand rather than hearing about it from others. When you are afforded the opportunity to see it for yourself, you develop your own opinions about the culture.

Having experienced diversity firsthand gives me the privilege to discuss it in full detail. The summer leading into my junior year of high school I went to Princeton University as part of the Junior Statesman of America Foundation. I was joined by high school students from America, the Middle East, China, Japan, and the Virgin Islands. We were all unique in the fact that we all had differences in food selections, native language and music preference. Despite the fact that we all had distinct differences, we also had some similarities and a common goal. One major similarity and common goal was that we wanted to pass the course we were taking.

Being exposed to diversity from different cultures gave me the opportunity to see that our

differences are what helped us reach our common goal. We were all given the same material by the same professor, the same textbook, and were taught in the same classroom. The difference was that we had different interpretations of the teaching based on our distinct cultures and background. Our differences allowed us to work together as a team so that we could comprehend the material and reach our common goal.

Because I have experienced diversity firsthand, I know how important it is in a college

community. I plan to bring my diversities to the college community to enhance their program. I desire to use my piece of the puzzle with the pieces from other students so that we can all work together towards our common goal of furthering our education.

Conversation Starters

When talking to recruiters

- What are qualities that you want your students to have?
- What programs do you offer for your students?
- Who is the most memorable person that came from your program?
- What do you define as success?
- Are there any minority student unions?

When talking to current students

- What made you decide to attend this college?
- Do you feel like your college is preparing you?
- How is campus life?
- If you could go through the process again, would you choose the same school?

When talking to administrators

- What is your advice for succeeding at this college?

When talking to alumni

- How did attending this college help you in your career?
- Do you feel like you connect with other alum?
- Has your college affiliation ever helped you in your field?

Getting to Know Your Roommate

Some things you may want to consider when choosing a roommate:

- Who's sleeping near the window?
- What amenities are you bringing?
- How should the room be set up?
- Are you a morning person or night person?
- Do you like loud music?
- Do you like a lot of people over at one time?
- Do you mind if we have company over?
- Does anyone have a boyfriend?
- Are we supplying toiletries for the entire room or just for ourselves?
- Who's going to sanitize the room on particular days?
- Are you messy or neat?
- What are we allowed to share and what's off limits?
- Who's buying the food/cookware? And who's able to use them?
- What types of things do/don't you like in a roommate?

These are just a few conversation starters to get the ball rolling. Answering these questions before moving in will help with the transition tremendously, as it allows everyone to be on one accord when you first move in. Addressing these things ahead of time means you'll have more time to spend getting to know your roommate and figuring out other things in your first year.

Gap Year Opportunities:

https://ocs.yale.edu/get-hired/gap-year-short-term-positions

This resource is pretty comprehensive and includes opportunities for graduates of all majors.

Scholarship Opportunities

Scholarships and Financial Aid:

Fastweb.com

This is one of the most widely used resources to find scholarships. These scholarships are usually reputable and the website is very user friendly. You simply put in your information, and it pulls up scholarships that you qualify for. This is a good resource because you can put in qualities such as being in a military family or having a disability and it will find scholarships tailored to you.

UNCF Scholarships

https://www.uncf.org/scholarships

This is an excellent source to obtain scholarships as a minority student as well as if you attend an HBCU. Additionally, you may become eligible for these scholarships while you are in college, so it is advantageous to keep an account updated with this website.

Corporate Scholarships

https://www.scholarships.com/financial-aid/college-scholarships/scholarships-by-type/corporate-scholarships/

NPHC Scholarships

Look for chapters in your hometown

Pretty much most if not all of the sororities and fraternities in the divine 9 offer some kind of scholarship for high school students. A good way to start looking for them is by finding a graduate chapter in your area and inquiring about scholarships. If you have any family that are members, you can ask them to help you as well. I was able to get a $1,200 through my aunt's graduate chapter which helped a lot.

Scholarship List:

The Agnes Jones Jackson Scholarship(Through NAACP)

Award Amount: Maximum of $2,000

Requirements:

High School, Undergraduate, or Graduate student

High School or Undergraduate GPA: 2.5

Graduate GPA: 3.0

How to apply:

http://www.poisefoundation.org/the-agnes-jones-jackson-scholarship/

You can apply for this scholarship from your senior year of high school through graduate school. So be sure to apply every year!

Gate Millennium Scholarship

Award Amount: Dependent on need but usually the cost to attend your institution including housing costs

Requirements:

High School Senior

Pell Grant Eligible

How to apply:

http://gmsp.org/

Rhodes Scholarship

Award Amount: Scholarship to attend Rhodes for study

Requirements:

Between the ages of 18 and 24

U.S.Citizen or U.S. resident with DACA status

How to apply:

http://www.rhodesscholar.org/applying-for-the-scholarship/

National Merit Scholarship

Award Amount:$2500

Requirements:

Take the PSAT before your third year of high school

U.S. Citizen

How to apply:

https://www.nationalmerit.org/s/1758/interior.aspx?sid=1758&gid=2&pgid=424

The National Merit® Scholarship Program is an academic competition for recognition and scholarships that began in 1955. High school students enter the National Merit Program by taking the Preliminary SAT/National Merit Scholarship Qualifying Test (PSAT/NMSQT®)—which serves as an initial screen of approximately 1.6 million entrants each year—and by meeting published program entry and participation requirements.

The link below is specifically for African-American Students:

https://www.nationalmerit.org/s/1758/interior.aspx?sid=1758&gid=2&pgid=433

Dell Scholars Program

Award Amount: $20,000

Requirements:

-Involved in AVID Program

-Need for financial assistance

-Graduating from accredited high school

-Minimum of 2.4 GPA

-Planning to enter a Bachelor's degree program

How to apply: Online Application

Website: http://www.dellscholars.org/

VSGA Scholarship Program

Award Amount: $3,000

Requirements:

-Good academic progress

-Active interest in golf

-Good character and citizenship

-Financial Need

-Virginia Resident

How to Apply: Online Application and Essay

Website: http://vsga.org/foundations/vsga-vip-scholarship-foundation/

Lee Jackson Educational Foundation Scholarship

Award Amount: $1,000-$10,000

Requirements:

-Virginia resident

-Junior or Senior in High School

-Plans to attend a four-year accredited US College

How to Apply: Online Application and essay regarding the life and history of Robert E. Lee and/or Thomas Stonewall Jackson

Website: http://www.lee-jackson.org/

Virginia State Bar Law in Society Essay Competition

Award Amount: $2,300

Requirements:

-Virginia Residents in high school

-Interest in law

How to Apply: Hypothetical Essay Contest

Website: http://www.vsb.org/site/public/law-in-society

National Peace Essay Contest

Award Amount: $1,000 $10,000

Requirements:

-High school students

-US Citizenship

How to Apply: Essay Contest

Website: http://www.usip.org/npec

National WWII Museum Student Essay Contest

Award Amount: $1,000

Requirements:

-No requirements

How to Apply: World War II Online Essay Contest

Website: http://www.nationalww2museum.org/learn/education/for-students/essay-contests/

Project Yellow Light/ Hunter Garner Scholarship

Award Amount: $2,000

Requirements:

-High School senior

-Submission of video with the "Don't text and Drive" message

How to Apply: Online Video Submission

Website: http://www.projectyellowlight.com/apply

We the Living Essay Contest

Award Amount: $25-$3,000

Requirements:

-10th, 11th, or 12th graders

How to Apply: Online Essay contest with We the Living Topic

Website: http://essaycontest.aynrandnovels.com/WeTheLiving.aspx?theme=blue

Ritchie-Jennings Memorial Scholarship

Award Amount: $10,000

Requirements:

-Full-time Students majoring in Business and Criminal Justice related majors

-Must enroll in at least 9 credit hours

How to Apply: Online Application

Website: http://www.acfe.com/scholarship.aspx

Discus Awards College Scholarship

Award Amount: $2,000

Requirements:

-Must demonstrate leadership/excellence in three of the following categories including: Academics, arts, athletics, community service, faith, government, green, technology, work, or another achievement.

How to Apply: Online Application

Website: http://www.discusawards.com/scholarship-info

Dutchcrafters Amish Furniture Heritage Scholarship

Award Amount: $500

Requirements:

-For high school seniors and college students

-Minimum GPA of 3.0

-Based on academic achievement, financial need and essay completion

How to Apply: Essay contest with a topic of using your heritage to shape your aspirations.

Website: http://www.dutchcrafters.com/heritage-scholarship

"Frame My Future: Scholarship Contest

Award Amount: $1,000

Requirements:

-Open to full-time undergraduate and graduate students

How to Apply: Submit an original creation with an image that expresses what you hope to achieve in your personal and professional life after college

Website: http://www.diplomaframe.com/contests/frame-my-future-scholarship-contest-2013.aspx

Tylenol Future Care Scholarship

Award Amount: Varies

Requirements:

-For students looking to have careers in the healthcare field

-Students with great leadership and academic excellence

How to Apply: Online Application

Website: http://www.tylenol.com/page.jhtml?id=tylenol/news/subptyschol.inc

Hispanic Scholarship Fund

Award Amount: Varies

Requirements:

-Student must be of Hispanic origin

-Students are given scholarship to aid in increasing collegiate graduates that are Hispanic

How to Apply: Online Application

Website: http://www.hsf.net/

Elks Legacy Award

Award Amount: $4,000

Requirements:

-Any child or grandchild of a living Elk who joined on or before 4/1/10

-Must be a high school senior

-Must have taken SAT or ACT

How to Apply: Online Application
Website: http://www.elks.org/ENF/scholars/legacy.cfm?CFID=28816866&CFTOKEN=85989262&jsessionid=84304a5b0bd8c7e690e7d23f5693601c4b76

AICPA Scholarship for Minority Accounting Students
Award Amount: Varies
Requirements:
-TBA
How to Apply: Online Application
Website: http://www.aicpa.org33/Career/DiversityInitiatives/Pages/smas.aspx

WyzAnt College Scholarship
Award Amount: Up to $10,000

Requirements:

-For high school Sophomores through college Juniors

How to Apply: 300 word essay about how you will use your education to impact others

Website: http://www.wyzant.com/scholarships/v3/Apply.aspx

Allen/Files Endowment

Award Amount: $1,000

Requirements:

-Virginia Resident

-From Augusta County, Staunton County. Or Waynesboro County

-Minimum 3.0 GPA

How to Apply: Online Application

Website: http://scholarship.epsilonsigmaalpha.org/

Dorothy Dyer Vanek Endowment

Award Amount: $1,000

Requirements:

-Virginia Resident

-Minimum 3.0 GPA or maximum 3.5

-Must major in Architecture or Interior design

How to Apply: Online Application

Website: http://www.epsilonsigmaalpha.org/scholarships-and-grants/scholarships/results/?state=Virginia

GRADUATE SCHOOL PERSONAL STATEMENT SAMPLE

Prompt: How did you become interested in clinical psychology?

I became initially interested in psychology when I was helping a friend who was considering suicide. I felt helpless because I couldn't understand his problems. I decided to learn more about human behavior and how to help those in need. I enrolled in a psychology course in order to understand more about what motivates people. I have become more interested in the field of clinical psychology during my four years at college.

In addition to my educational experience, I actively pursued work experience in psychology related fields. I worked as a resident assistant in one of the dormitories during my junior and senior year. In this role, I encountered students who had problems relating to their family, depression, suicide, alcohol, and drugs. I attained an internship position during my senior year at a psychological rehabilitation facility dedicated to helping injured individuals to deal with and overcome their situations. I witnessed counseling of both clients and their families, and I learned to administer and score several psychological tests used in clinical assessment. My work experience has proven to me how much more I need to learn before I can attain my goal of becoming an accomplished researcher and teacher.

I became interested in research as a sophomore when I enrolled in a research class. By the time I graduate, I will have presented a total of ten papers on a variety of topics at undergraduate research conferences. My experience with the first study, an examination of mood effects on time perception, led to other research endeavors on topics including student evaluation of faculty, academic integrity, and comparisons of personality profiles of brain injured individuals. The relevance of two of these projects, academic honesty and student evaluation of faculty, led me to present my results at two college conferences. As an undergraduate, I have learned the importance of working closely with members of the faculty. A great deal can be accomplished by working with someone who is already an expert in the field.

I have become firmly committed to the beliefs that the most appropriate way to answer "real world" questions is through basic research and that these answers should be communicated in a professional manner to those audiences who can benefit most from them. My undergraduate experiences have inspired me to continue my education in graduate school so I can further my research and make a meaningful contribution to the field of psychology.

Made in the USA
Columbia, SC
15 April 2019